Ainsley
xx.

The Publisher wishes to acknowledge the following owners of the dogs in this book: Bill Alexander, Nancy Brayton, Alan Cole, Joseph M. Edwards, Margaret English, Jane A. Firestone, Stephen Heaven, Susan C.T. Hill, Roy Hunter, Donald James, Ruth Jeram, Bob Langendoen, Roberta Laufer, Sue Lavoie, Robert and Nancy Mc Farland, James Moses (agent), Penelope and David R. Neicho, Missy Parker, R.V.T., Pat Paterson, Joseph Petracca, Charlotte Schwartz, Charlotte Solich, Regina and David Steiner, Becky Stewart, Virginia Stewart, Nanci A. Takash, Gladys Taylor, William Tipton, Jamie Walker, Kathleen A. Walker, Janet Borowy Weisman, Robin K. Wescher, Denise Wood, Donna L. Youngblood.

Photographers: Tracy Atkins, Genie Adams, Jena Bremy, Margaret English, Karen Ervin, courtesy of Fleabusters, Rx for Fleas, Inc., Isabelle Francais, Carol Hayes, Susan Hill, Lois Hunter, Judy Iby, Corrina Kamer, Bob Langendoen, Sue Lavoie, Sandra Marshall, Maria Martins (Unique Image), Penny Neictto, Celia Ooi, Mark Parker, Missy Parker, courtesy of Janet Quilligan, R.V.T., Charlotte Schwartz, Vince Serbin, Judith Strom, Penny Sullivan, Nanci Takash, Karen Taylor, Angela Thompson, Chris Van Der Westhuizen, Donna Youngblood. Drawings by John Quinn.

The author acknowledges the contribution of Judy Iby for the following chapters: Sport of Purebred Dogs, Identification and Finding the Lost Dog, Traveling with Your Dog, and Health Care for Your Dog.

Distributed in the UNITED STATES to the Pet Trade by T.F.H. Publications, Inc., One T.F.H. Plaza, Neptune City, NJ 07753; distributed in the UNITED STATES to the Bookstore and Library Trade by National Book Network, Inc. 4720 Boston Way, Lanham MD 20706; in CANADA to the Pet Trade by H & L Pet Supplies Inc., 27 Kingston Crescent, Kitchener, Ontario N2B 2T6; Rolf C. Hagen Inc., 3225 Sartelon St. Laurent-Montreal Quebec H4R 1E8; in CANADA to the Book Trade by Vanwell Publishing Ltd., 1 Northrup Crescent, St. Catharines, Ontario L2M 6P5 ; in ENGLAND by T.F.H. Publications, PO Box 15, Waterlooville PO7 6BQ; in AUSTRALIA AND THE SOUTH PACIFIC by T.F.H. (Australia), Pty. Ltd., Box 149, Brookvale 2100 N.S.W., Australia; in NEW ZEALAND by Brooklands Aquarium Ltd. 5 McGiven Drive, New Plymouth, RD1 New Zealand; in Japan by T.F.H. Publications, Japan—Jiro Tsuda, 10-12-3 Ohjidai, Sakura, Chiba 285, Japan; in SOUTH AFRICA by Lopis (Pty) Ltd., P.O. Box 39127, Booysens, 2016, Johannesburg, South Africa. Published by T.F.H. Publications, Inc.

MANUFACTURED IN THE
UNITED STATES OF AMERICA
BY T.F.H. PUBLICATIONS, INC.

A New Owner's Guide to GERMAN SHEPHERDS

Charlotte Schwartz

Contents

1996 Edition

6 • Dedication

6 • Preface

7 • Acknowledgments

8 • History of the German Shepherd Dog

20 • Portrait of the German Shepherd Dog
Physical Appearance

34 • Standard of the German Shepherd Dog

46 • Working German Shepherd Dogs

The German Shepherd is descendant from sheepdogs, and the herding instinct remains inherent in the breed today.

The German Shepherd Dog is a natural beauty who has achieved a high level of popularity around the world.

64 • Reflections on a German Shepherd Dog

German Shepherds need plenty of exercise and room to roam.

66 • Selecting Your German Shepherd Dog
Before You Buy •
Age • Socialization • Registration •
Picking a Puppy

92 • Caring for Your German Shepherd Dog
Feeding • Exercise • Grooming

German Shepherds are athletic and coordinated, performing very well at agility trials and the like.

104 • Housebreaking Your German Shepherd Dog
Types of Training • Puppy's Needs • Housing • Control Schedule • Six Steps to Successful Training • Canine Development Schedule • Obedience Training

120 • Sport of Purebred Dogs
Conformation • Canine Good Citizen • Obedience • Tracking • Agility • Schutzhund

128 • Identification and Finding the Lost Dog
Finding the Lost Dog

130 • Traveling with Your Dog
Trips • Air Travel • Boarding Kennels

136 • Dental Care for Your Dog's Life

142 • Health Care for Your Dog
The First Check Up • The Physical Exam • Immunizations • Annual Visit • Intestinal Parasites • Other Internal Parasites • Heartworm Disease • External Parasites • To Breed or Not to Breed

159 • Suggested Reading

160 • Index

German Shepherd puppies are playful and spunky.

DEDICATION

To all the German Shepherds I have known and to those who have yet to cross my path. My own species is enriched by yours, and I am most grateful.
Charlotte Schwartz

PREFACE

"State its purpose and offer acknowledgments." Those were the words uttered to me by a wise and wizened editor who was trying to teach me how to write a book many years ago.

The purpose of this book is to lay the cards on the table regarding the German Shepherd Dog. In it I've tried to honestly present his strengths, his weaknesses, his character, and his worthiness of having a singular book written about him. But most of all, I've tried to share with my readers my own feelings and enthusiasm for the breed as well as my concerns for it in the future.

ACKNOWLEDGMENTS

I'd need at least a chapter to list all those who have come forward to help create this book. People who shared their stories, people who took some fine quality photographs of their dogs, people who have had a lifetime of experiences living with and training this admirable breed, and responsible breeders–those guardians of that most indefinable facet of German Shepherddom, the nature of the beast.

To all of them, I offer a sincere and humble Thank You. You helped make my work so much easier, so much more delightful, and I hope, so much more meaningful to its readers.

If I live to be one hundred, I will never forget the first Shepherd I lived with. His name was Perro and he was born before I was. My early childhood was dominated by this huge dog that never let me go out of his sight. He was strong, patient, tender and comforting. The day he died was my first experience with death. And every death of a loved one since then has been subconsciously equated to his passing. Only a few have surpassed the profundity of his loss to me.

Finally, to my editors, Jaime Gardner and Andrew DePrisco, I extend my heartfelt gratitude. They believed I could write fairly of the German Shepherd. They guided my thoughts on the matter and my work. I salute you both!

Now, dear reader, enjoy this volume and weigh carefully whether you are worthy of sharing your life with such a grand companion.

HISTORY of the German Shepherd Dog

Welcome to the world of the German Shepherd Dog. Writing a book about a specific breed of dog can be hazardous to an author's reputation. She can overexaggerate the finer qualities of the breed, promise the reader more than the breed is capable of giving, or, in an attempt to control one's enthusiasm, downplay genuine breed qualities thus making the written word sound like it came from an encyclopedia. None of this is so when writing about German Shepherds!

The German Shepherd gracefully embodies the old sheepdog prototype and is ideally suited for the task of herding.

German Shepherd Dogs are possibly the most honest breed of dog the world has ever known. A well-bred, mentally and physically sound German Shepherd is never an imposter. In a world where fakery in both man and dog has become commonplace, the German Shepherd does not put on airs, either those of hostility or of silliness. Consequently, to write about German Shepherd Dogs and maintain credibility, this author must be nothing less than honest.

This purity of personality and purpose comes from its very beginnings as a specific breed of dog. Possessing the knowledge of how the German Shepherd was originally developed will serve you well in understanding what it should and should not be.

Though the true age of the breed is not known for sure, the German Shepherd is one of the oldest and one of the most versatile of all shepherd breeds.

Back in the 19th century, a compelling need by shepherds for a dog to help guard their flocks produced a diverse collection of dogs with a wide variety of behavioral and physical characteristics. Yet all of these dogs exhibited a willingness to protect sheep. They were categorized as "sheepdogs."

In 1891, a group of sheepdog enthusiasts formed the Phylax Society in order to standardize this motley collection into a breed of native German dogs with fixed structure and characteristics. However, the Society was short-lived and disbanded in 1894. But one man, Captain Max von Stephanitz, maintained his belief that the qualities of intelligence and ability seen in so many of these dogs could be the foundation for a new breed of sheepdog.

In 1899 von Stephanitz saw a dog called Hektor

Linksrhein at a dog show. The cavalry officer was so impressed with Hektor that he purchased the dog on the spot. Shortly thereafter, he, together with a group of other enthusiasts, formed Verein fur deutsche Schaferhunde. The organization, known throughout the world today as the SV, was to become the largest individual breed club in the world and is credited with establishing the new German Shepherd Dog as a specific breed.

Von Stephanitz promptly renamed his new dog Horand v. Grafrath. Horand would eventually sire Hektor v. Schwaben who became a Sieger, or Grand Champion, in 1901. During that same year von Stephanitz assumed the position of president of the breed club he helped to form, and from that point on the German Shepherd Dog's future was assured.

Horand was a medium sized dog with more than adequate bone, a wedge-shaped muzzle, and an excellent temperament. Fortunately he passed these traits to his progeny. His son, Hektor, was out of a female named Mores Plieningen, reportedly of sheepdog and wolf heritage.

In his definitive work, *The German Shepherd Dog, its History, Development and Genetics* (K & R Books, Ltd., Leicester, England. First published 1976.), Dr. Malcolm

Rich dark pigment is desirable in all German Shepherds. Notice the particularly dark face on this handsome young male.

Willis reminds us that Mores is, in all probability, related to every German Shepherd alive today.

Intelligent and aware, the German Shepherd makes an excellent companion and protector.

As history moved into the 20th century, von Stephanitz realized how the needs of mankind were progressing, too. No longer would herding be the dominating criteria for the breed as it had been for so long. Instead, the age of industrialization would make new demands for dogs that were adaptable to cities, increased human populations, and ever-expanding governmental organizations and activities.

Controlled breeding programs and stringent testing of the German Shepherd's abilities produced dogs that met the new needs. By World War I, German Shepherds were ready to go to war in the roles of messenger, search and rescue, sentry and patrol dogs.

Properly socializing puppies with humans, especially children, is essential to avoid shy or overly-aggressive dogs.

At this point, German Shepherds were not well-known in the United States, but that was about to change. The first Shepherd to enter this country was a female named Mira v. Offingen. She was imported in 1906 and the granddaughter of Hektor v. Schwaben.

During World War I, American soldiers stationed in Europe witnessed firsthand the intelligence, physical ability and stamina demonstrated by the German Shepherds of Germany. Many of these soldiers returned home with a dog that they purchased in Europe.

Then, in the late 1920s, several dogs that had earned Siegers in Germany were imported to America. Their bloodlines, coupled with those of Mira, were to forever influence the American-bred German Shepherd Dog.

Though the dogs were instantly admired by breeders and exhibitors alike, the breed's name caused great concern. The word "German," whether used outright or implied, was inference enough to create strong feelings of hostility in all the allied countries. The United States was no exception. Thus Americans decided to call the breed Alsatian Wolf Dogs, named for the area of Alsace-Lorraine near the German-French border from which some of the dogs had originated.

The German Shepherd is popular throughout the world. This handsome male enjoys a look around the beach at the Tasman Sea in Australia.

This, however, caused a new problem. The word "wolf" created an undesirable image because many people feared the breed saying the dogs were part wolf. The truth of the matter is, though there was almost certainly wolf blood in the earlier dogs, so many generations had evolved since the deliberate breeding to a wolf back in the 1800s that the term "wolf" referred only to the greyish-sable color of some German Shepherds.

Though the German Shepherd Dog Club of America was established in 1913, the breed waited through a

Although the importance of physical soundness cannot be overstated, breeders today also concentrate on a friendly and outgoing temperament.

series of name changes and verbal conflicts before being awarded a name. Finally in 1977, the name German Shepherd Dog was officially given to the breed and it remains so in America and most countries to this day.

Shortly after World War I, the breed found its way to Great Britain and a breed club was formed to govern what the British called the Alsatian Wolf Dog. In 1924, a second organization joined forces with the first and the name was changed to become the Alsatian League and

Club of Great Britain. The change was made when a majority of the members chose to bring the name in line with similar clubs in other countries.

During this time the potential of the breed was recognized by all the allied forces, and soon German Shepherds were being trained for armed forces duty in America and Europe. In addition, the breed's ability to act as Seeing Eye dogs for the blind in both the United States and Britain was being utilized with great success. German Shepherds, with their intelligence and trainability, were the breed of choice for this highly responsible work.

A nine-week-old German Shepherd puppy already possesses the alert and inquisitive expression of the breed.

Following the end of World War II, the German Shepherd in the United States experienced a roller coaster ride of first admiration and then contempt and finally back up to the level of respect and esteem he deserves. Regrettably, this seesawing occurred as a result of human intervention and a total disregard for genetic backgrounds of individual dogs.

When people began to realize the potential of this breed, especially for personal protection, some individuals saw another kind of potential for themselves–money. Realizing that Shepherds usually produce large litters, greedy individuals recklessly bred any German Shepherd to any other German Shepherd. The resulting puppies were sold for exorbitant prices when they were advertised as "good protection dogs." Unfortunately the public, not taking the time and effort to learn more about the breed, ended up with highly unsuitable pets. Hip dysplasia (an abnormality of the ball and socket joint of the hip), missing teeth, monorchidism (only one testicle descended into the scrotum), and incorrect ear carriage were all structural problems that were intensified by poor breeding practices.

Fear-biters, shy or overly aggressive dogs, destructive neurotics, dogs that were incapable of bonding with owners, and even untrainable dogs were seen regularly in humane societies and animal shelters. These dogs were eventually euthanized, but only after much suffering by their former owners and the dogs themselves.

However, greedy individuals cared little for the outcome of the puppies they produced. They thought only of the profits their efforts would bring. Unfortunately this situation stamped the German Shepherd as vicious, mean, untrustworthy, often physically unsound, and extremely undesirable. German Shepherd popularity plummeted.

The German Shepherd is a hardy, long-lived breed. This ten-year-old Shepherd is a beautiful example of the breed.

By the 1960s this complex problem was addressed simultaneously on several fronts. Dr. Wayne Riser, from the University of Pennsylvania in Philadelphia, joined with several other veterinary orthopedic physicians to study hip dysplasia and the means to control it. He was instrumental in developing the OFA, the Orthopedic Foundation of America. Following a comprehensive study of genetics and a research program, the OFA established a radiological method of determining hip dysplasia in individual dogs and certifying those free of it as being of breeding quality.

The German Shepherd Dog Club of America offered a Register of Merit, or ROM, title to sires and dams whose progeny proved their show worthiness. Obviously a dog with major faults would not be considered of show quality and, if exhibited, would not be judged favorably

over more correct specimens.

Though considered controversial by some, the ROM was an attempt by the parent club to demonstrate that good parents produce good puppies. This was certainly a step in the right direction.

This, together with the German SV, Class I (dogs with no faults) and Class II (dogs with minor faults), has served to send a clear message to all concerned including breed enthusiasts and prospective puppy buyers that physical and mental soundness with "an abundance of temperament" must be the criteria from which a German Shepherd is chosen as either a companion or a working dog.

Today, breeders around the world are working hard to ensure that the breed does not fall into disfavor again. Reputable breeders not only scrutinize the backgrounds of breeding age sires and dams, they question interested buyers as to how their puppies will be raised and for what purpose. They frequently follow up on the development and progress of their dogs' progeny. In short, they're policing the breed and making certain that the German Shepherd remains for all time an honest dog.

Since the German Shepherd has been popular for decades as a purebred companion dog and show dog,

At one year of age this German Shepherd adolescent is well trained and ready to protect its owner.

many excellent resources are available on the breed for further study. One of the very earliest is the classic *This Is the German Shepherd* by Captain William Goldbecker and famed enthusiast Ernest H. Hart, published in 1955 by T.F.H. Publications. This title is no longer available except through collectors. Other excellent sources include *The German Shepherd Dog,* also by Ernest H. Hart, and *The World of the German Shepherd Dog* by all-breed judge and author Anna Katherine Nicholas. Both these titles are available from T.F.H. and can be found at a local pet-supply outlet or book store.

Proper ear carriage is important in the German Shepherd. At thirteen weeks of age, this puppy's ears are beginning to stand.

German Shepherds usually have large litters. This litter of ten sable puppies was bred in Australia.

PORTRAIT of the German Shepherd Dog

From extreme dedication and toughness, coupled with the ability to make split-second decisions, to quiet patience and the ability to be extremely flexible, the German Shepherd Dog is a dozen other breeds of dog all in one. A German Shepherd Dog is not number one at anything, but he's number two at everything!

German Shepherds should be exercised in a variety of places. These dogs are getting their day's exercise romping in the Tasman Sea in Australia.

Sighthounds are faster runners; some terriers are fiestier and will challenge anything that threatens them; Giant Schnauzers and Great Danes, for example, are larger; some toy breeds have keener hearing; some scenthounds have superior olfactory systems. However, no other breed of dog combines all the traits and attributes like those of the German Shepherd Dog. And he's been proving this claim since his earliest ancestors demonstrated their all-around abilities.

A German Shepherd Dog is agile, graceful, quick, and endowed with more stamina than possibly any other breed. He's willing to rest by the side of a wheelchair all day, walk at a snail's pace alongside a person with crutches, run beside a jogger for hours on end, or herd sheep from sunup to sundown. He is well-muscled, an athlete whose body structure is designed for endurance.

The German Shepherd is a fiercely loyal dog who wants only to be with his master. This black long-coated Shepherd nuzzles up to his master for a perfect picture.

Aside from his uniqueness of conformation, the German Shepherd possesses certain indefinable qualities that are almost impossible to describe yet easy to see when they're present. For example, his noble character can be seen in his expression. He's a fiercely loyal individual and only wants to be with his master. Thus he tends to keep one eye on his owner a lot more than most breeds whose focus seems to wander.

Though he rarely makes overtures of friendship toward strangers, he is fearless yet willing to accept those whom his owner deems acceptable. Should the owner be hesitant about befriending someone, the dog will pick up this hesitation and stand his ground. His expression will alter instantly to suggest that the stranger best not come any closer.

He's powerful enough to pull a small child out of the way of oncoming traffic when he senses danger. He's intelligent enough to learn that other pets must be accepted when the owner chooses to share his time with them. And, providing he receives a fair share of attention and the training necessary to permit him to function in a multi-pet environment, the German Shepherd will accept other pets. He will even tolerate baby pets, such as kittens and puppies, often growing quite protective of them as well.

Due to his natural tendency of protectiveness, he must be exposed to children, adults, other pets, etc. from an early age. He must learn that, as devoted to you as he is, there is also a big world out there and he must fit into it peacefully. Fortunately, the German Shepherd is intelligent enough to learn these lessons and accept others.

In summary, the German Shepherd Dog can be formidable yet gentle, assertive yet passive, serious yet fun-loving, aloof yet friendly. He can be happy living outdoors and joining his human companions indoors in the evening, or he can adapt to life in a small

Due to the breed's natural tendency of protectiveness, this toddler couldn't have a better friend or guardian than a German Shepherd.

apartment. Regardless of his living arrangements, he must receive daily exercise in addition to regular walks for elimination. One must never forget that he is first and foremost an athlete, both in body and mind. And as such, his prowess must be challenged regularly and exercised daily.

German Shepherds love to join their human companions on bicycle rides. Make sure your dog has access to water during vigorous exercise.

In my role as an animal behaviorist and dog obedience instructor, I have seen more German Shepherds become behavior problems to their owners than any other breed of dog. And in every case, the reason for the dog developing unwanted behaviors was

German Shepherds adore the great outdoors. These three white Shepherds enjoy the fresh and wide open spaces of the Rocky Mountains in Idaho.

In addition to regular walks for elimination, German Shepherds must also receive daily exercise. This pack explores a dirt road in the outback joined by a Boston Terrier friend.

caused by a lack of stimulation and exercise.

It is virtually impossible to take a highly intelligent and physically active individual, whether it be man or dog, and expect him to do nothing without paying a costly price for such quiescence. This fact brings up a vital point in the matter of German Shepherd ownership.

German Shepherds are not the ideal breed of dog for everyone. If a person is rarely home, has little or no time to devote to the dog's well-being, does not have the facilities or inclination to provide exercise, training, and play for the dog, that individual would be wise to consider another breed of dog.

Though the German Shepherd is extremely adaptable to its owner's lifestyle, he must be given an adequate amount of attention and direction on a daily basis. The dog can wait all day while his owner is at work without suffering separation anxiety and becoming destructive, but he needs to know that, at the end of the day, he and his owner will spend time interacting and exercising together.

Sometimes this can mean playing fetch in the living room when storms rage outdoors. At other times it can mean long walks in the woods, jogging, even running across fields or along sandy beaches together. Agreeable with almost anything the owner has in mind, the German Shepherd is saying, "As long as I can be doing something with you, boss, I'll be happy."

The secret to the successful

The secret to success for German Shepherd ownership is doing things together. This Shepherd runs a fine track with its owner.

ownership of a German Shepherd is *doing things together*. We must never forget that the German Shepherd comes from a long (hundreds of years old) line of working dogs: dogs that ran all day across fields as they herded sheep and guarded flocks; dogs that never tired or experienced boredom; dogs that were genetically disposed to working with their masters, not away from them.

These genes still run through the German Shepherd today, and must never be discounted as immaterial or unimportant. They are what makes the Shepherd what he is and always will be, the epitome of function. In a world that offers several hundred breeds of dog for potential companionship, the German Shepherd is truly a unique breed and, as such, must be owned with respect, pride, and an awareness of the dog's needs.

The German Shepherd is well-muscled, an athlete whose body structure is designed for endurance.

Physical Appearance

In the United States, Canada, Australia, South Africa, Great Britain and Germany, national breed clubs have set the standards of perfection that determine what is and what is not acceptable in the physical conformation of the German Shepherd Dog. It's with these breed standards that we should familiarize ourselves before purchasing a dog.

At four months of age, this black and tan female puppy's ears just don't seem to fit her head yet.

Basically there are three types of color: black and tan saddle, sable, and solid black. Coat colors range

On black and tan Shepherds the darker colors are usually seen on the saddle and around the face.

from beige, gold, tan, reddish brown, grey, black and silver to combinations of these. White Shepherds are disqualified in the conformation ring but can be shown in Obedience and Herding Trials.

Generally speaking, the darker, richer shades are preferred over the washed-out, more faded ones. Whatever the coat color, the darker shades are seen on the back, along the sides of the dog, on the tail and around the face.

Lighter colors are seen on the head, legs, chest, shoulders and feet. Bloodlines often determine the amount of dark or light on individual dogs. Whatever the shades of black and brown, spots or streaks of white are unacceptable.

Saddles are usually of the black and tan combination, though black and gold or black and silver can be seen. The saddle marking is where the black appears as a saddle over the back and down the sides of the dog. It breaks abruptly at the shoulders, but carries down the top of the tail and up the neck. The contrast in coloration is more prominent in saddled dogs.

The best way to describe a sable coat is to say that the grizzled saddle of the sable dog is less noticeable in

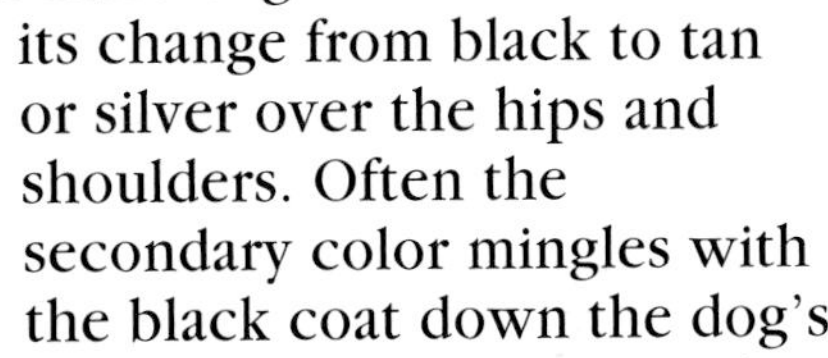

its change from black to tan or silver over the hips and shoulders. Often the secondary color mingles with the black coat down the dog's back and along the spine as well as making the saddle itself almost disappear.

In the sable coat the secondary color mingles with the black coat down the dog's back and spine as well as making the saddle itself almost disappear.

Coat types range from short and coarse to long and soft. Though the short-coated Shepherd is preferable, long-coated dogs have recently become eligible for showing in the breed ring.

Whether the dog is short-coated or long-coated, the German Shepherd should have a double coat. The outer coat is coarse in texture with the under-coat being dense and fine. The combination of these two types of hair is essential to providing protection against rain, cold and debris. The coarser outer coat resists water and foreign matter while the dense, soft undercoat retains the dog's body heat in cold climates. Be assured that regardless of the type of coat you choose, it will require some care though not like that of many other breeds.

The eyes of the Shepherd can range anywhere from yellow to dark brown. They are to be almond-shaped and never protruding. The eyes, often referred to as the windows of the soul, are what give the German Shepherd the expression of intelligence and alertness.

Ear carriage and size are equally contributive to the Shepherd's expression. Ear size should be in proportion to the head size, never so small that the dog appears to have cropped ears yet never so large that they make the head seem diminutive.

The ears are carried erect from the outer corners of the head with the rounded tips pointing straight upward. Lop ears in puppies are often seen and will usually correct themselves as the dog matures. Sometimes, breeders will tape up a lop ear to aid the muscle at the base of the ear to strengthen as the puppy grows.

The size and carriage of the ears are equally contributive to the German Shepherd's expression.

The German Shepherd head must, first and foremost, fit the body to which it belongs. For example, a large male must not have a small, feminine head. And a female with a coarse, heavy-muzzled head is to be penalized. The length of the black muzzle must also be in concert with the size of the head and the overall impression of the body. A small, delicate head would be out of proportion on a large, heavy-boned dog just as a smaller, finer-boned dog would look ridiculous with a large head.

There should be an almost smooth line from the top of the skull to the tip of the black nose with only a minor dip at the stop (point along top of muzzle just below the eyes).

At maturity the dog must have a full set of 42 teeth set in a scissors bite. Overshot jaws (where the top teeth are way out in front of the lower ones and sometimes referred to as "buck teeth") or undershot

jaws (where the bottom incisors protrude out in front of the upper ones such as seen in Bulldogs) are considered serious faults. A scissors bite, on the other hand, is where the top teeth come down over the lower teeth with the inside of the top teeth barely touching the outside of the bottom teeth.

Puppies frequently have "floating jaws," which means the bite seems to fluctuate between scissors, overshot and undershot. However, by the time the puppy is full grown a proper bite and full complement of teeth is expected.

The German Shepherd's body should be longer than he is tall from the withers (top of the shoulders) to the ground. The chest is deep and the forelegs are shorter than the hind legs, which should be well-angulated. A correct shoulder assembly and powerful hindquarters are what give the dog endurance for long hours of travel.

His rib cage should be flattened at the sides, not rounded and barrel-like as in many other breeds. The back should not be excessively long and should slope slightly downward toward the hindquarters or croup. The tail should be long and straight, ending below the hock joint (the joint directly above the foot and below the knee).

Shepherd weight varies with bloodlines and genders. Mature males usually weigh between 75 and 95 pounds, females between 65 and 85 pounds. At birth, Shepherd puppies weigh in at between 8 and 14 ounces.

A good example of the German Shepherd gait. Note that the dog appears to be almost floating over the ground.

The overall appearance of a German Shepherd is that of an alert, muscular, graceful, well-balanced dog. His gait is often called a flying trot and, when seen from the side, appears to be floating just above the ground. Studying the dog in motion, it sometimes appears that only one foot at a time is in contact with the ground. Puppies are a lot less coordinated and trot along often picking up each foot as if it weighed a ton. Their gait is erratic and unpredictable, but will improve as their motor skills develop.

German Shepherds are always alert. This pair awaits their next activity at a summer camp for dogs and owners.

The overall appearance of the German Shepherd is that of a graceful, well-balanced dog.

STANDARD of the German Shepherd Dog

The standard of a breed is the criterion by which the appearance (and to a certain extent, the temperament) of any given dog is made subject, as far as possible, to objective measurement. Basically the standard for any breed is a definition of the perfect dog, to which all specimens of the breed are compared; the degree of excellence of the appearance of a given dog for conformation show purposes is in direct proportion to the dog's agreement with the requirements of the standard for its breed. Breed standards are always subject to change through review by the national breed club for each dog, so it is always wise to keep up with developments in a breed by checking the publications of your national kennel club.

The number one show dog of all time is Champion Altana's Mystique owned by Jane A. Firestone.

The following is a version of the American Kennel Club standard for the German Shepherd Dog.

General Appearance–The first impression of a good German Shepherd Dog is that of a strong, agile, well-muscled animal, alert and full of life. It is well balanced, with harmonious development of the forequarter and hindquarter. The dog is longer than tall, deep bodied, and presents an outline of smooth curves rather than angles. It looks substantial and not spindly, giving the impression, both at rest and in motion, of muscular firmness and nimbleness without any look of clumsiness or soft living. The ideal dog is stamped with a look of quality and nobility–difficult to define, but unmistakable when present. Secondary sex characteristics are strongly marked, and every animal gives a definite impression of masculinity or

The head of the German Shepherd is noble and cleanly chiseled. The expression is keen, intelligent and composed.

femininity, according to its sex.

Size, Proportion, Substance–The desired ***height*** for males at the top of the highest point of the shoulder blade is 24 to 26 inches; and for bitches, 22 to 24 inches. The German Shepherd Dog is longer than tall, with the most desirable ***proportion*** as 10 to $8^1/_2$. The length is measured from the point of the prosternum or breastbone to the rear edge of the pelvis, the ischial tuberosity. The desirable long proportion is not derived from a long back, but from overall length with relation to height, which is achieved by length of forequarter and length of withers and hindquarter, viewed from the side.

Head–The ***head*** is noble, cleanly chiseled, strong without coarseness, but above all not fine, and in proportion to the body. The head of the male is distinctly masculine, and that of the bitch distinctly feminine. The ***expression*** keen, intelligent and composed. ***Eyes*** of medium size, almond shaped, set a little obliquely and not protruding. The color is as dark as possible. ***Ears*** are moderately pointed, in proportion to the skull, open toward the front, and carried erect when at attention, the ideal carriage being one in which the center lines of the ears, viewed from the front, are parallel to each other and perpendicular to the ground. A dog with cropped or hanging ears must be *disqualified*. Seen from the front the forehead is only moderately arched, and the ***skull*** slopes into the long, wedge-shaped muzzle without abrupt stop. The ***muzzle*** is long and strong, and its topline is parallel to the topline of the skull. ***Nose*** black. A dog with a nose that is not predominantly black must be *disqualified*. The lips are firmly fitted. Jaws are strongly developed. ***Teeth***– 42 in number–20 upper and 22 lower–are strongly developed and meet in a scissors bite in which part of the inner surface of the upper incissors meet and engage part of the outer surface of the lower incisors. An overshot jaw or a level bite is undesirable. An undershot jaw is a *disqualifying fault*. Complete

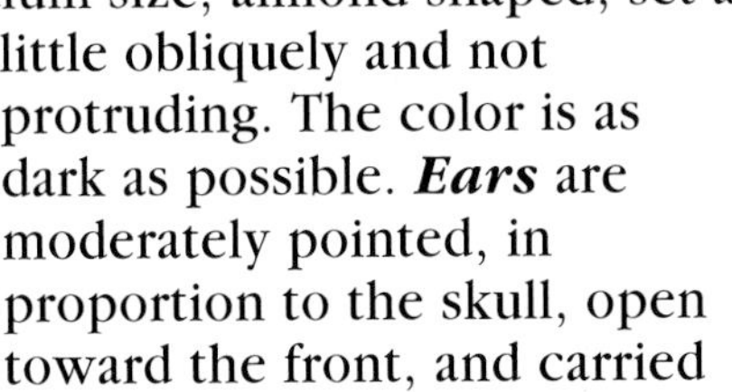

The muzzle should be long and strong with its topline parallel to the topline of the skull. The nose is always black and the lips are firmly fitted.

dentition is to be preferred. Any missing teeth other than first premolars is a *serious fault.*

Neck, Topline, Body—The ***neck*** is strong and muscular, clean-cut and relatively long, proportionate in size to the head and without loose folds of skin. When the dog is at attention or excited, the head is raised and the neck carried high; otherwise typical carriage of the head is forward rather than up and but little higher than the top of the shoulders, particularly in motion. ***Topline***— The ***withers*** are higher than and sloping into the level back. The ***back*** is straight, very strongly developed without sag or roach, and relatively short. The whole structure of the ***body*** gives an impression of depth and solidity without bulkiness. ***Chest***—Commencing at the prosternum, it is well filled and carried well down between the legs. It is deep and capacious, never shallow, with ample room for lungs and heart, carried well forward, with the prosternum showing ahead of the shoulder in profile. ***Ribs*** well sprung and long, neither barrel-shaped nor too flat, and carried down to a sternum which reaches to the elbows. Correct ribbing allows the elbows to move back freely when the dog is at a trot. Too round causes interference and throws the elbows out; too flat or short causes pinched elbows. Ribbing is carried well back so that the loin is relatively short. ***Abdomen***

The German Shepherd should be fearless and self-confident, always willing to accept those his owner deems acceptable.

The ideal German Shepherd is stamped with a look of quality and nobility that is difficult to define but unmistakable when present.

White Shepherds are disqualified in the conformation ring but can be shown in Obedience and Herding trials.

firmly held and not paunchy. The bottom line is only moderately tucked up in the loin. ***Loin***– Viewed from the top, broad and strong. Undue length between the last rib and the thigh, when viewed from the side, is undesirable. ***Croup*** long and gradually sloping. ***Tail*** bushy, with the last vertebra extended at least to the hock joint. It is set smoothly into the croup and low rather than high. At rest, the tail hangs in a slight curve like a saber. A slight hook–sometimes carried to one side–is faulty only to the extent that it mars general appearance. When the dog is excited or in motion, the curve is accentuated and the tail raised, but it should never be curled forward beyond a vertical line. Tails too short, or with clumpy ends due to ankylosis, are *serious faults*. A dog with a docked tail must be *disqualified*.

The German Shepherd is longer than tall with the desired proportion being 10 to 8. The length is measured from the breast bone to the rear edge of the pelvis.

Forequarters–The shoulder blades are long and obliquely angled, laid on flat and not placed forward. The upper arm joins the shoulder blade at about a right angle. Both the upper arm and the shoulder blade are well muscled. The forelegs, viewed from all sides, are straight and the bone oval rather than round. The pasterns are strong and springy and angulated at approximately a 25-degree angle from the vertical. Dewclaws on the forelegs may be removed, but are normally left on. The ***feet*** are short, compact with toes well arched, pads thick and firm, nails short and dark.

Hindquarters– The whole assembly of the thigh, viewed from the side, is broad with both upper and lower thigh well muscled, forming as nearly as possible a right angle. The upper thigh bone parallels the shoulder blade while the lower thigh bone parallels the upper arm. The metatarsus (the unit between the hock joint and the foot) is short, strong and tightly articulated. The dewclaws, if any, should be removed from the hind legs. Feet as in front.

Coat– The ideal dog has a double coat of medium length. The outer coat should be as dense as possible, hair straight, harsh and lying close to the body. A slightly wavy outer coat, often of wiry texture, is permissible. The head, including the inner ear and foreface, and the legs and paws are covered with short hair, and the neck with longer and thicker hair. The rear of the forelegs and hind legs has somewhat longer hair extending to the pasterns and hock, respectively. *Faults* in the coat include soft, silky, too long outer coat, woolly, curly and open coat.

Color— The German Shepherd Dog varies in color, and most colors are permissible. Strong rich colors are preferred. Pale, washed-out colors and blues or livers are *serious faults*. A white dog must be *disqualified*.

Gait— A German Shepherd Dog is a trotting dog, and its structure has been developed to meet the requirements of its work. *General Impression*— The gait is outreaching, elastic, seemingly without effort, smooth and rhythmic, covering the maximum amount of ground with the minimum number of steps. At a walk it covers a great deal of ground, with long strides of both hind legs and forelegs. At a trot the dog covers still more ground with even longer stride, and moves powerfully but easily, with coordination and balance so that the gait appears to be the steady motion of a well-lubricated machine. The feet travel close to the ground on both forward reach and backward push. In

When trotting, the German Shepherd's hindquarters reach far under, passing the imprint left by the front foot.

order to achieve movement of this kind, there must be good muscular development and ligamentation. The hindquarters deliver, through the back, a powerful forward thrust which slightly lifts the whole animal and drives the body forward. Reaching far under, and passing the imprint left by the front foot, the hind foot takes hold of the ground; then hock, stifle and upper thigh come into play and sweep back, the stroke of the hind leg finishing with the foot still close to the ground in a smooth follow-through. The over-reach of the hindquarter usually necessitates one hind foot passing outside and the other hind foot

At a trot the German Shepherd covers a great deal of ground, moving powerfully but easily with coordination and balance.

The German Shepherd Dog varies in color, and most colors are permissible. Here are examples of a solid black and a black and tan saddle.

passing inside the track of the forefeet, and such action is not faulty unless the locomotion is crabwise with the dog's body sideways out of the normal straight line. ***Transmission***–The typical smooth, flowing gait is maintained with great strength and firmness of the back. The whole effort of the hindquarter is transmitted to the forequarter through the loin, back and withers. At full trot, the back must remain firm and level without sway, roll, whip or roach. Unlevel topline with withers lower than the hip is a *fault*. To compensate for the forward motion imparted by the hindquarters, the shoulder should open to its full extent. The forelegs should reach out close to the ground in a long stride in harmony with that of the hindquarters. The dog does not track on widely separated parallel lines, but brings the feet inward toward the middle line of the body when trotting, in order to maintain balance. The feet track closely but do not strike or cross over. Viewed from the front, the front legs function from the shoulder joint to the pad in a straight line. Viewed from the rear, the hind legs function from the hip joint to the pad in a straight line. Faults of gait, whether from front, rear, or side, are to be considered *very serious faults*.

Temperament– The breed has a distinct personality marked by direct and fearless, but not hostile, expression, self-confidence and a certain aloofness that does not lend itself to immediate and indiscriminate friendships. The dog must be approachable, quietly standing its ground and showing confidence and willingness to meet overtures without itself making them. It is poised, but when the occasion demands, eager and alert; both fit and willing to serve in its capacity as companion, watchdog, blind leader, herding dog, or guardian, whichever the circumstances may demand. The dog must not be timid, shrinking behind its master or handler; it should not be nervous, looking about or upward with anxious expression or showing nervous reactions, such as tucking of tail, to strange sounds or sights. Lack of confidence under any surroundings is not typical of good character. Any of the above deficiencies in character which indicate shyness must be penalized as *very serious faults* and any dog exhibiting pronounced indications of these must be excused from the ring. It must be possible for the judge to observe the teeth and to determine that both testicles are descended. Any dog that attempts to bite the judge must be *disqualified*. The ideal dog is a working animal with an incorruptible character combined with body and gait suitable for the arduous work that constitutes its primary purpose.

Disqualifications

Cropped or hanging ears

Dogs with noses not predominantly black

Undershot jaw

Docked tail

White dogs

Any dog that attempts to bite the judge

If you are planning a show career for your German Shepherd, you must study the breed standard and learn how to show your dog to its best advantage.

WORKING German Shepherd Dogs

The role the German Shepherd Dog plays in modern life is almost endless. Undoubtedly, the biggest demand for German Shepherds today is for companions. However, this isn't to say that German Shepherds are not used in working situations.

As war messengers they must be able to go from their own handler to another soldier over rough and often hazardous terrain, usually in the black of night and often past enemy troops, to deliver secret messages of critical nature. Once the delivery is made, the dog must then, upon command, return to his handler over the same treacherous route. The key to this type of performance is reliability. The German Shepherd has proved beyond a doubt that he is trustworthy and capable of getting the job done, often at great risk to his own life.

Officer Stephen Heaven looks on as Callan practices jumping hurdles in preparation for a demonstration for the Queen.

Have you seen a guide dog at work with his blind owner on the streets of your home town? If so, you must have marveled at the dog's ability as he guided his human partner in and around obstacles, across busy highways, up and down stairs and through crowds of shoppers without showing fear or aggression toward others nearby. German Shepherd guide dogs are faced daily with making decisions

Officer Stephen Heaven and Callan were partners on the Thames Valley Police Department in England. The two served together for five years.

regarding the safety of their owners, all without guidance or help from someone else.

In both cases, the dogs must exhibit a tremendous amount of self-confidence and the ability to maintain prolonged focus on a task, as well as perform their jobs using an extraordinary amount of self-control.

A German Shepherd can be trained to simulate a tornado turned loose in a shopping center or a bull gone wild when, with courage and determination, he scatters an ugly crowd-threatening violence. However, in the role of a search and rescue dog, he can play the part of a soft, gentle kitten when he lays down beside a frightened child lost in the forest.

He carries within his genes the ability to be all these

things and more, providing he is trained appropriately. From herding sheep to guarding a sleeping baby in a carriage, the German Shepherd is truly the most versatile breed of dog the world has ever known.

Let's look now at some examples of German Shepherd Dogs in both work and recreational roles. We'll see the diversity of the breed and how, around the world, German Shepherds serve their owners in a multitude of capacities.

Devil, a police dog with the Fort Meyers Police Department in Florida, waits at the top of the A-frame obstacle for the command to come down.

In the small condominium community of Marlow, the homes were built in the shape of a "U." Each faced a common parking lot directly across the street from the edge of the picturesque countryside.

The dark, moonless night promised peaceful sleep to the residents of the little English village. But on the outskirts of town, the night was about to erupt into a war zone.

In one of the center homes, a man, driven by alcohol and a predisposition to violence, turned his inner fury toward his wife. By one o'clock in the morning, he was battering his mate and turning objects in the home into flying missiles.

Local police were called to quell the disturbance. In addition, Officer Stephen Heaven was dispatched to the scene with his partner, Callan, a German Shepherd Dog. That's when the suspect's mood turned vicious.

When Officer Heaven and Callan reached the footpath outside the home, the suspect emerged from the house armed for battle. He carried a

Officer Keith Tipton and Devil keep an eye on each other as they prepare to go on duty.

crossbow, a sabre, a knife and an airgun. When he saw Callan, he threatened to kill the dog but then he promptly took off in a run.

Heaven and Callan followed right behind. As he ran, the man dropped all his weapons except the knife and the crossbow. Eventually, he stopped and turned to aim at the officer with his crossbow. When he did, Officer Heaven sent Callan to subdue the man. "Generally local police officers in England do not carry weapons," explains Heaven. "I was no exception. However, as a K-9 Corps officer, I knew that Callan would serve as my weapon if and when I needed one." Callan, an outstanding police dog dedicated to his master, launched himself at the suspect before the man had a moment to prepare for the attack. Callan bit the man several times and forced him to the ground. Officer Heaven backed up his dog and together they subdued the man.

The moment Heaven had control of the situation, Callan backed off and stood watch, ready to reenter the fight should the suspect decide to resist. Other local officers joined Heaven and the suspect was arrested.

On a bookshelf behind Officer Heaven's desk there is a plaque that reads, "Commendation for Professionalism and Courage in overpowering and arresting a violent, intoxicated man armed with a crossbow, a sabre, a knife and an airgun."

Callan served as Heaven's partner for five years until the dog developed a heart condition and died. He was followed by Dirk who served with Heaven for three years until the officer suffered a back injury while on duty and was forced to retire from the Thames Valley Police Department after 15 years of service.

In the small seaside city of Fort Myers on the Gulf Coast of Florida, another German Shepherd Dog spends his life apprehending felons and protecting his owner, Police Officer Keith Tipton. Devil, a nine-year-old black and tan Shepherd, was imported from Holland as a police K-9 Corps dog in 1989.

One night, Tipton was attempting to arrest a man who was on crack/cocaine. Suddenly, the suspect turned on the law man and tried to take his gun by punching the officer in the face and wrestling him to the ground.

At that point, Devil leaped from the patrol car and attacked the suspect. After delivering several bites to the suspect, Devil subdued the man in a ditch where Tipton was able to gain control once again. In the meantime, Devil kept a steady watch over the suspect while Tipton handcuffed the man.

Obedience Trial Champion Noonmark's Quincy Jones, UDX, Ber. CD, Can. OTCH, CGC, waits on the pause table during an agility session.

When not on patrol, Devil lives at home with Tipton, his wife, two young children and a little mixed breed dog named Missy. Some time ago, Devil sired a litter of puppies. Now, one of the males from that litter is being trained to replace Devil when retirement day comes. His schooling includes protection, tracking and search work, marine law enforcement, and public relations duty with school children.

Now let's meet some of the German Shepherds I call the "all-rounders." These dogs are usually purchased as companions and live in private homes with their owners.

While the puppy is growing up, the owner enrolls in a beginner's obedience class to teach his dog good manners and gentle behaviors. Once exposed to the learning process and the ritual of practicing together, the owner discovers that both he and his dog enjoy working together.

They learn about dog shows, obedience trials, tracking, agility competitions, and a dozen other activities in which they can become involved. The idea of continuing their education and developing new skills is exciting for both.

One such dog is Quincy and his master is Nancy Brayton of Mount Holly, New Jersey. Quincy, a long-coated, black German Shepherd, was purchased in 1987 to replace a female German Shepherd who had recently passed away.

Nancy, an obedience instructor and owner of a dog training school, started Quincy's schooling with a puppy class where he was taught basic manners and how to pay attention. After all, learning to focus attention on one's master is the beginning of learning many behaviors in the future. He was also socialized with other dogs and people and learned that weekly classes and short, daily practice sessions were a normal part of life.

By graduation day, Quincy had learned to love working with Nancy. The next step was a regular obedience class. From there, he moved up to the novice level, prepared for entering obedience trials and earned a Companion Dog title in 1989.

The road to stardom began when Nancy realized,

Lucas is on his way to earning a Herding Dog Intermediate title. Here he moves the sheep into a grazing area.

during the course of pursuing a CD title, that Quincy had the potential to become a great obedience champion. By 1992 Quincy had earned the coveted Utility Dog Title, but he wasn't yet ready to retire from obedience trial competition.

Lucas jumping into the pen to force the flock of sheep out and onto a road. Being able to tend a flock includes protecting the sheep from traffic.

In 1994 he became Obedience Trial Champion Noonmark's Quincy Jones, UDX. He is the first German Shepherd in American Kennel Club history to earn a Utility Dog Excellent title. He is also the first herding dog to earn that title.

By November of that year he was pronounced Obedience Victor by the German Shepherd Dog Club of America. In addition, Quincy traveled to Bermuda and Canada where he earned CD and Obedience Trial

Lucas herding sheep out of the pen. He began herding 20 sheep and can now easily handle 50.

Jed, Dorsey, Obe, and Socks are all Search and Rescue dogs of the Intermountain S & R Dog Association in Idaho.

Champion titles respectively. Quincy and Nancy have stamped their names and record of achievements into the history of German Shepherds in America. Today, Quincy and Nancy still enter special shows and competitions for fun. When not training, Quincy travels to schools and retirement homes to visit children and the elderly as a Canine Good Citizen dog. All this from a puppy who was purchased as a companion!

Let's change the pace and look at five-year-old Lucas, a black and tan Shepherd who lives with owner Margaret English in Purdys, New York. Lucas shares his home with five other dogs ranging from a Chihuahua to a Golden Retriever. And much to his credit, he copes with this "family" peacefully!

Lucas began life with Margie when she volunteered to raise puppies for Guiding Eyes for the Blind, an organization in Yorktown Heights, New York. Soon after joining Margie's family, he began basic obedience lessons while, at home, he learned how to get along with other dogs and people. "But," recalls English, "when he was tested by the Guiding Eye people at 14 months of age, he didn't make the cut for additional training and life as a guide dog. By that time, he and I were very attached so I decided to keep him myself, although I had no idea what we could do together to make our companionship meaningful."

"Then one day I attended a clinic to learn what herding trials were all about. I took Lucas along and that's when we were bitten by the herding bug." English and Lucas were soon enrolled in private herding lessons.

Flash, a Search and Rescue dog, and Bob Langendoen search through the rubble of a mudslide in Puerto Rico.

He began working 20 sheep and now easily handles up to 50. He learned to "tend" a flock, which means he was taught to keep them together, prevent them from wandering off alone, protect them from traffic, and move them from place to place.

Not long ago, Lucas entered an AKC Herding Trial and earned his first leg toward a Herding Dog Intermediate title. He must earn two more legs to qualify for it. The test begins with a flock of sheep in a pen. The owner opens the gate to the pen and orders the dog to keep the sheep inside. The dog then stands in the open gateway and prevents them from getting out.

Next the dog is sent around to the side of the pen and ordered to jump a 30-inch fence into the milling sheep. That drives the sheep out of

Even Search and Rescue dogs need a little R&R. Here Socks and owner Sue Lavoie take some time out.

Elise boards a helicopter during a Search and Rescue training mission in Maine.

the pen. Now comes the hard part. Lucas must move the flock down a road, keeping them on the road and off the grassy sides, not an easy thing to do. No sheep may wander off, run too far ahead, lag behind, or stop to graze. Soon they come upon an intersection. Lucas must stop the flock and search for oncoming traffic.

Suddenly a car approaches. Lucas must maneuver himself so that he stays between the car and the sheep at all times. While this is happening, Margie is standing on the sidelines calling out commands to him.

Finally, when he's proven that he can protect the flock, Lucas is ordered to bring the sheep back down the road to the original pen. Though Margie is allowed to call commands to Lucas, she may not touch the dog while he's working.

This German Shepherd in South Africa is a loyal companion and service dog to her owner who has only one arm.

All this takes between 20 and 30 minutes and the dog is allowed as much time as needed to get the job done. It's obvious from Lucas' demonstration of tending a flock that he, indeed, does it correctly. But what about the times when he is not tending sheep? What does he do then?

"He just hangs around the house with the rest of us," smiles Margie. "He definitely needs something to do. That's what makes him such a good friend the rest of the time."

Finally, let's look at some German Shepherds and the lives they live with their owners in Idaho as members of the Intermountain Search and Rescue Dog Association. Interestingly, most of these dogs were abused or misunderstood by previous owners who found they just couldn't cope with them. What the original owners didn't realize was that the dogs needed to have a purpose in life, not just a home.

Amidst the unspoiled beauty of the Rocky Mountains, this family of two people, Sue Lavoie and Bob Langendoen, and four German Shepherds is the quintessential search and rescue family. As Langendoen said, "We spend all of our free time and most of our money on being "Ambassadors of Goodwill."

A German Shepherd Dog of the Military Working Dog Agency at Lackland Air Force Base in Texas searches a series of boxes for drugs or explosives.

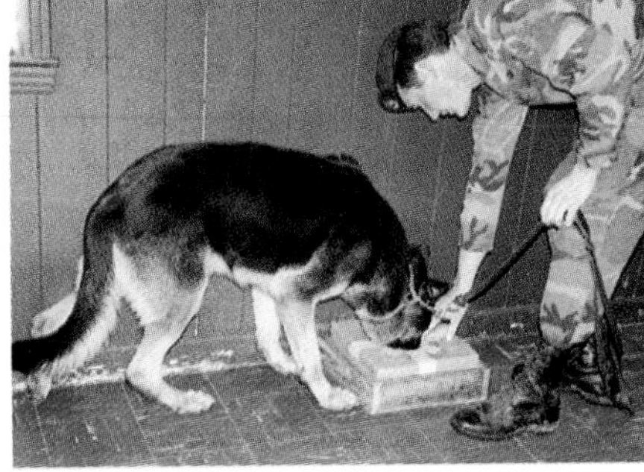

The work of search and rescue dogs is grueling. It requires years of patient training for the dog to learn to locate and indicate the scent of humans, both dead and alive. The environment is often hostile, the weather frequently miserable.

Not all German Shepherd Dogs have what it takes to succeed at search and rescue work. They must be driven by high energy, ambition, sociability, curiosity, self-confidence and a strong drive. These qualities are essential in the search and rescue dog because, once he's trained, he will frequently be asked to work hour after hour, day after day, to find a lost person.

The Lavoie/Langendoen Shepherds meet all these qualifications. Jed and Dorsey, both white Shepherds, lend their years of experience and proven abilities to perfecting the skills of the younger members of the team, Socks, black and tan, and Obe, another white dog. They're all recognized as superb search dogs by those in the field as well as law enforcement officials who've worked with them.

Langendoen's first German Shepherd, a white dog named Flash, lived $15\frac{1}{2}$ years. During that time Flash ran searches from Maine to Virginia, New Jersey to the Rocky Mountains. He searched for people buried in the mudslide disaster in Puerto Rico in 1985; for lost children, hikers and fishermen; and for fugitives escaped from the law. Stories of his searches have appeared in newspapers and books.

German Shepherds can still participate and excel in herding events. Nordwind's Sundance Scamp, CDX, PT, CGC, waits to start a Herding Trial.

When Lavoie purchased her first German Shepherd, Elise, in 1981, she says she "did everything wrong." Sue bought on impulse, chose a puppy that was only five weeks old, and did no research into the puppy's breeding or background.

Despite the poor beginning, Sue persisted and gave the puppy a lot of love while she studied dog behavior and training. Then, they began working together while Sue continued her quest for knowledge through seminars and clinics.

Many German Shepherds hold Schutzhund titles. Here Ryker Von Polarstern, SchIII, nails the helper.

Elise earned Companion Dog and Tracking Dog titles from the American Kennel Club. Later, she was trained in protection and search work and served alongside Flash for many years.

Elise lived for 14 years and was Sue Lavoie's most loyal and devoted friend. "I wouldn't trade those years with her for anything in the world," says Sue. "Now I've got Socks and she's turning out to be a clone of Elise!"

Both owners were introduced to search and rescue work through the American Rescue Dog Association (ARDA) in New Jersey. ARDA, incidentally, is the only search and rescue organization that uses German Shepherd Dogs exclusively in their work. Members believe that the German Shepherd is the ideal breed for this work because it demands so much of the dog in intelligence, stamina, trainability and dedication to performance.

Other Shepherds make their mark in their owners' memories with less public recognition yet just as indelibly. A young dog named Duke lives with and protects his ten-year-old master who suffers from cerebral palsy. A dog named Apache accompanies his mistress to her office from which she runs a busy plumbing business. A dog named Anka rides in the cab of a large pickup truck with her master, a construction company owner. And in the years since Anka has been

One thing a dog is taught in Schutzhund training is to bark before it bites.

going to job sites, her owner has never had a tool stolen from the truck bed!

These and thousands more like them around the world bring joy, security and pride to their owners every day. Regardless of the country of residence or the job they perform, all these German Shepherds have one important thing in common. They live and work with owners who recognize and appreciate the dogs' needs to be functional. Just being a pet who lays around the house or in the backyard is not enough for a German Shepherd.

These stories serve to demonstrate the versatility of this fascinating breed. In addition to his loyalty, intelligence and self-confidence, he's a noble animal that portrays a loftiness of spirit and an excellence of character. A few among them have exhibited these characteristics under some extremely difficult conditions and survived to be called regal.

Dorsey, CD, CGC, searches the banks of the Big Wood River in the Rocky Mountains for a missing fisherman.

REFLECTIONS on a German Shepherd Dog

Something recently came my way that was so uplifting, so moving that I wanted to share it with my readers. Rather than dwelling on the sorrow of losing a friend, I saw in it a tribute to the essence of the German Shepherd Dog that was so profound it begs to be celebrated.

It does not speak of specifics or details. It does not attempt to teach or exalt. It merely shares with the reader the thoughts of a German Shepherd Dog owner who was infinitely sensitive to the value of her dog's companionship and how it helped mold her own life.

Melissa Parker is a breeder, obedience instructor, and a Registered Veterinary Technician in Texas. She is also a wife and the mother of two sons. For the past 11 years she has been the owner of a German Shepherd named Thunder.

Thunder hits the mark of a fine German Shepherd Dog.

Thunder passed away on April 10, 1995. Shortly afterward, Ms. Parker wrote a eulogy honoring his life rather than lamenting his death. And I was privileged to receive a copy of it. Now I'd like to share it with you.

A Tribute To Thunder

Today the spirit of my guardian angel was set free. He was a truer, more constant friend than I have ever known or will know again.

Thunder stood ever vigilant by my side as I passed through the sunshine and shadows of eleven years. He taught me more about dogs, about love, and about how to be a friend than all the words in all the books I have ever read. He was my best friend, my counselor, protector, confidante, playmate, workmate and soulmate. On another plane of existence, we were integral parts of each other. I am diminished with his passing for he takes a piece of the best part of me, my joie de vivre, with him. I pray that my work with other owners and their best friends will be a fitting tribute in honor of him for it is he who blessed me with this particular joy.

He has blazed a trail before me to a place in the Great Beyond where there is no cruelty, no loneliness, no pain or suffering, no sadness or strife, and it is solace indeed to know that I will walk by his side again one day in that beautiful place. Until we meet again, I shall forever mourn the loss of the gentle spirit and great comforter that he was.

At age 11 years Thunder still presented an image of strength and dignity.

SELECTING Your German Shepherd Dog

If I were allowed just one sentence to offer as advice to the potential puppy buyer, it would be: "Do your homework!" By that I mean one must investigate, inquire, and inspect. Investigate the background of the breed or breeds of your interest. Read all the material you can find related to those breeds. Most pet shops have a good selection of books on dogs.

A good way to investigate the breed is to go to dog shows in your area. Seek out the people who are exhibiting German Shepherds and ask questions.

Go to dog shows in your area. Most shows are advertised in local newspapers, on television and radio. Seek out the people exhibiting your breeds of interest and ask questions. Most of all, observe the dogs and how they react to the stress and excitement of crowds and other dogs. Do the dogs appear to be having fun, or do they seem anxious, nervous, even aggressive toward other dogs and strangers?

Talk to local dog trainers, obedience instructors, and veterinarians. And, by all means, listen carefully to what they have to say. For example, a person may say that a particular breed "isn't the easiest to train" when

German Shepherd owners must have time for their dogs, especially when they are puppies. This young German Shepherd chases after its owner.

In Kindergarten Class puppies and owners are taught to enjoy learning together. This is another place prospective German Shepherd owners can go to find out about the breed.

what they really mean is, "This breed is tough. It takes a firm handler to get and maintain control of this breed." Or they may comment that their breed isn't crazy about cold weather. This translates to, "My dog loves the heat and refuses to go out during the winter," which means you could have housebreaking problems when the weather turns cold.

Then evaluate for yourself whether or not you and your loved ones are the right type of people to cope with that particular breed. If you're not, this is the time to look at some other breeds of dogs.

Veterinarians will be able to tell you what health

problems they most often see in your breeds of interest. Some physical problems are easy to manage and cause the dog little or no suffering. Others are more serious, cause a great deal of suffering, and are often life-threatening.

Keep in mind that all the people mentioned above have no financial interest in sharing information with you. Owners, dog show exhibitors, veterinarians, trainers and instructors are not directly rewarded by giving you advice. You may ultimately seek their professional help, but initially they want only to communicate their findings with genuinely interested parties.

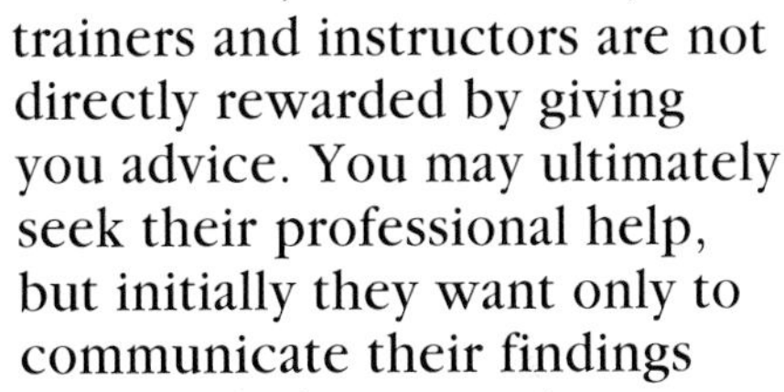

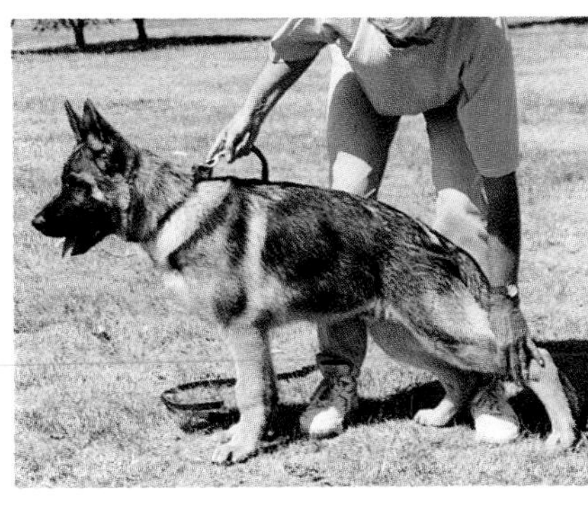

Before you purchase a puppy, make sure you are aware of the breed's conformation and know what to look for in a good representative.

Next talk to breeders. These are the people responsible for producing puppies representative of a particular breed of dog. If the puppies grow up not looking and acting like the breed they represent, the breeder's credibility is to be questioned.

Reputable breeders care very much about the puppies they produce. They are also proud of their dogs' progeny and want only to see their puppies get into good homes where the breed will flourish and serve as good public relations examples to the world.

Talking with breeders is usually not a one-way conversation. Most will gladly answer your questions, volunteer more information than you thought necessary, and show a great deal of interest in you and your reasons for wanting a dog of their breed.

In my years as a breeder, I turned away more than

one person as a potential puppy buyer. Whether I felt the person was unable to care for the puppy properly, or the person and his family were just too unfit to own a dog, I never hesitated to be courteous yet firm in my suggestion for them to either consider a different breed or another type of pet all together.

Perhaps those suggestions didn't make me new friends, but at least I felt good knowing that I had saved one of my puppies from a regrettable fate. And, as a breeder, my allegiance to my breed had to come first.

Another excellent source of information is the owners of some of the breeder's puppies. A reputable breeder is more than happy to refer you to some of their puppy buyers. And those buyers are always delighted to have you meet their dogs and share their feelings about their choice of pet.

Your investigation should include looking at photos of some of the dogs produced and shown by the breeder. You'll be able to get a good idea of size, color and type from these pictures.

Ask to see the pedigrees of the sire and dam of the puppies in question. The breeder will also introduce you to the dam of the litter and, if available, the sire as well.

Pedigrees are the history of bloodlines that, combined through generations of breeding, go into

This puppy class is being introduced to a child's pool. Note that the German Shepherd pups are the first ones in!

making up the dogs you see today. I always find it fascinating that often a puppy will develop into a carbon copy of a grandparent, so study the pedigrees and get familiar with bloodlines.

When they are ready to meet the world, puppies will be difficult to contain. These puppies are begging for new experiences.

You're getting closer to a decision about what breed of dog will best fit into your lifestyle and bring you joy as a companion. There are perfect people and homes for almost every breed of dog. It remains for you to decide if the German Shepherd is the right breed for you.

Before You Buy

Next, you need to locate the source of your potential new German Shepherd. Sometimes people purchase a dog

At four weeks of age, puppies are already moving around on their own quite well. Here they are being introduced to children and the great outdoors.

from a breeder who lives many miles away. This entails a series of letters, phone calls, photos and much discussion, not to mention that the seller should come highly recommended by someone you know and trust who also know the seller and his or her reputation within the breed.

Before you are ready to purchase a dog, you have even more details to work out. Let's take a look at some of the additional decisions you'll have to make before you write that check.

What sex of dog you buy will be among your first considerations. Females are usually gentle and enjoy staying close to home. Males are usually more curious and tend to

It is a good idea, if possible, to see the dam of the puppy you are purchasing. This proud mother guards and cares for her babies with total devotion.

When choosing a German Shepherd puppy, pick the one that comes to you readily.

explore the neighborhood more unless they are controlled. In addition, males are usually larger than females with heavier bone structure and often more abundant and denser coats.

Either sex can and should be neutered unless the dog is destined for a show ring and a career of reproduction. Spaying a female and neutering a male has many good results.

It makes the dogs mellower, more content to be with family and home, and easier to control. On the other hand, it does not take away from their protective instincts or ability to work.

Intact males are interested in females throughout the year. Intact females usually come in season twice a year for 21 days each season and thus need to be confined if you don't want them getting pregnant. They can also become finicky and irritable at those times. Lastly, they are extremely interested in male dogs of any breed during periods of estrus.

Breeding puppies should be left to the breeders. Contrary to popular belief, breeding puppies rarely generates large profits for the breeder. The cost of stud fees, maintaining a breeding female before, during and after breeding, and raising a litter of puppies is extremely high. Much higher than most people care to admit! Worming and vaccinating the puppies before they go to new homes is costly as well. Worming and immunizing puppies against distemper, hepatitis, parainfluenza, parvo and coronavirus before the puppies can be sold is mandatory in many states.

If an emergency arises, such as the need for a Caesarean section, the expenses become astronomical. This does not take into account the risk to the mother's life or her future ability to produce puppies and, in most cases, cannot be predicted in advance.

AGE

When people think of acquiring a new dog, they most often think of a puppy–a baby puppy. One that's between eight and 12 weeks of age. Although the dictionary defines a puppy as a young dog less than one year of age, I break that down even further.

I consider a puppy to be between the ages of eight and 20 weeks of age. An adolescent is from five to 12

At five weeks of age Savant and Dama are ready to meet the world, but not yet ready to go to their new homes.

months of age, and an adult is a dog over one year of age.

There are advantages and disadvantages to purchasing a German Shepherd in each of these categories, which you need to know before you can make a well-informed decision about the dog that's going to be a part of your family for many years.

Puppies are like raw clay. You begin with good quality material and mold it to suit your lifestyle and wishes. Since it hasn't lived long enough to develop bad habits, you can begin teaching it good habits right from the start.

It's fascinating to observe the growth and development of a youngster, whether a human or a dog. Seeing how they learn, mature and discover the world around them can be extremely exciting and rewarding.

A 22-day-old German Shepherd puppy displays bright eyes and a pink tongue–a true picture of health!

On the minus side, there's puppy teething and chewing, housebreaking, jumping on people and furniture, and sometimes excessive barking and digging to contend with. You should plan on crate training your puppy and be prepared to take him outdoors frequently until his urinary system is fully developed at about six months of age. This means getting up several times during the night and serving breakfast at 6 AM! And little puppies need to be fed three times a day.

Because they're teething and often have aching gums, little puppies love to chew on soft things, especially your hands and ankles. If you have toddlers or tiny babies to think of, large breed dogs can be a problem if they are in the same stages of development as the human babies. You will need to provide your puppy with safe and effective chew devices to satisfy his chewing needs. For puppies, the Gumabone® products are probably best, due to their softer composition.

Small breed puppies are in danger of being sat on by toddlers and are sometimes injured in the process. Further, toddlers don't always understand your attempts to train the puppy and frequently undo whatever it is you're trying to accomplish. Think about all these things before you decide on the age of puppy you'll buy.

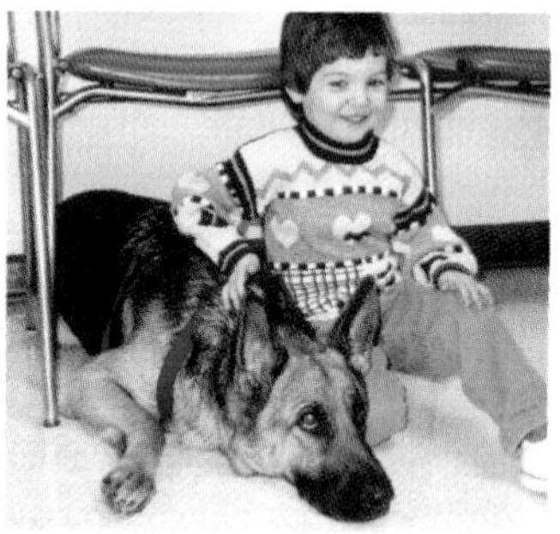

If you plan to acquire an adult German Shepherd as a family pet, make sure that the dog has been exposed to small children.

Adolescent dogs have the early housetraining behind them and are usually pretty reliable when it comes to not having accidents in the house. Though there are still some developmental stages to go through, the adolescent usually understands what "no" means and chews less because his permanent front teeth are in, but he still faces the emergence of molars that often cause some serious chewing on hard items. If you realize this, you can provide pacifiers for constructive chewing and teach him not to use your coffee table legs as chew toys. The safest and most provenly effective canine chew products are the Nylabone® and Gumabone® pacifiers.

The adolescent is still young enough to form a bond with you if you make an effort. He is eager to participate in your lifestyle yet occasionally needs reminders to use good manners. You'll be able to witness the transformation from gangly teenager with long spindly legs that seem to go in every direction at once to graceful adult. All these stages of development are exciting to observe and participate in.

Whether you choose a baby puppy or an adolescent, you should plan on taking the dog to an obedience class for some basic training. Not only will he learn good manners and simple commands such as sit, stay, down, and come, but he will build that bond with you as his master. This is the foundation from which all you do together for the rest of his life will come. It's worth the time and effort!

Now let's consider purchasing an adult German Shepherd. First, you need to know that adults for sale are rare compared to the availability of puppies. Occasionally you may see an advertisement in a newspaper for an adult, but you must seriously question the reasons why this dog is for sale. Sometimes people sell adults because of behavior problems that you will not be able to correct. In this case, you'll be stuck with someone else's problem!

Once in a while, a

At four months of age this puppy faces the emergence of molars causing the need to chew on hard things. Provide pacifiers for constructive chewing, such as Nylabones®.

reputable breeder will offer to sell an adult because the dog's show career has ended, possibly because of age or physical problems. The breeder will usually spay or neuter the dog and look for a good pet home for it.

With an adult dog, there are no growing-up problems to face, but you must be prepared to allow the dog enough time to adjust to his new home with you. This requires a lot of patience on your part, but it can be most rewarding.

Adult dogs are ideal purchases for older people with limited physical abilities and stamina. Providing the dog is well-mannered, the adult dog can better fit into a quieter, slower lifestyle than a young puppy.

Young families with active children do not make ideal homes for an older dog if the dog has had no prior experience with growing children and all that it implies. If, however, an adult dog is coming from an active family that included young children, the dog will likely learn to love his new young masters and fit in well. It will be up to you to determine whether or not your home situation is similar to that from which the adult dog is coming.

The cost of an adult dog is often much less than it is for a puppy or adolescent. The purpose in placing an adult dog is usually for the betterment of the dog so price is rarely a consideration. The bottom line that the seller will be looking at is whether or not her adult dog will fit well into your home and family unit.

SOCIALIZATION

Regardless of the age of the German Shepherd you choose to purchase, one of the most important factors in choosing a new dog is how you perceive that dog when you first meet it and spend some time getting to know it. We've all heard the story about the person who was searching for a dog, found one and, upon meeting the animal, discovered that he and the dog were made for each other.

However, a dog of any age, even a puppy, that runs from you, hides in a corner, or in any way acts frightened of your presence, is not an ideal candidate no matter how appealing he may look. The key, therefore, to preventing this problem of the dog's shyness in the first place is socialization. And socialization must begin with the breeder long before you

Socialization is important to the development of puppies. The process should begin at a young age with the littermates.

ever meet the dog.

As a matter of fact, the older a dog is before socialization begins, the more difficult it is for the dog to adjust to new situations and surroundings. Some dogs, deprived of early socialization, are never able to adjust to new homes and people, and are doomed to live out their lives in their original home never knowing how wonderful and full life can be.

Socializing a puppy beginning when he is four or five weeks of age starts with letting family members and friends hold and play with the puppy. He is subjected to a wide variety of situations and environments such as a backyard, a kitchen, a park, a ride in the car just for fun, or a visit to meet children and other pets. In other words, the young puppy is exposed to a cross section of life as he will know it when he becomes an adult.

Once the puppy is settled in his new home, the same procedure must be repeated regularly in new surroundings with all new people and pets. If this socialization is approached on a basis of fun and the reward of positive attention, the puppy's confidence level will grow so he can cope with life and all it has to offer.

That's one of the major advantages to kindergarten and beginner's training classes. The exposure to new

Each one of life's lessons is important. This dam disciplines one of her puppies who tries to wander away from the litter.

dogs, people and experiences assures a well-balanced adult who is sure of himself and his family.

Even the older dog needs to be socialized with other dogs and people.

If you're considering an adolescent, make sure that he has been properly and adequately socialized during his formative months (between two and five months of age). You can tell if this is so by observing how he handles meeting you and your family.

So look for the dog, either puppy or adult, who accepts you and appears interested in interacting with you. Needless to say, an adult who shows signs of lacking socialization should not be considered for purchase. A full grown German Shepherd, for example, is a large powerful dog and a fearful one may be prone to fear biting. Regardless of the reason for biting, a bite is a bite and must be considered a serious matter.

I have known a number of people who have taken non-socialized dogs, German Shepherds included, into their homes because they felt sorry for the dogs. In every case, the people vowed to acclimate the dogs to their homes and family.

This, however, was never accomplished and frequently ended when the dog either ran away or bit someone and was euthanized as a final solution. In all those cases, the people involved were heartbroken when they realized they could not change behavioral patterns that had been formed in the developmental stages of the dog's life.

In short, socialization or the lack of it serves to determine the path a dog's behavior will follow for his entire life. That being the case, which incidentally has been proven by scientific studies, socialization affects you as much as the dog.

REGISTRATION

At this point let's address the matter of kennel clubs, registrations, pedigrees, and what they mean to you. Kennel clubs are registering bodies for purebred dogs. In addition, they maintain records such as championship titles, sporting event degrees, and offspring produced by individual dogs registered with them.

For example, when an American Kennel Club-registered sire (father) and dam (mother) produce a litter of puppies, the breeder registers the litter's birth with the AKC. Each puppy in that litter is then given an individual registration application form that goes with the puppy to the new owner.

This floppy-eared ten-week-old puppy is ready to go to his new home. Make sure to ask for a registration application when you pick up your new pup.

In a recent public information ad, the American Kennel Club wrote, "If you buy a purebred dog that you are told is eligible for registration with the American Kennel Club, you are entitled to receive from the seller an application form that will enable you to register your dog.

"If the seller cannot give you the application, you should demand and receive full identification of your dog in writing, signed by the seller, consisting of the breed, the registered names and individual registration numbers of your dog's sire and dam, your dog's date of birth, the name of its breeder and, if available, its AKC litter number.

"Don't be misled by promises of 'papers' later."

The new owner selects a name for his puppy and registers that name with the AKC which, in turn, gives the puppy his own individual registration number. That number stays with the dog for life. The number is

also used to trace the ancestors of the dog and create a pedigree, or genealogical record. The pedigree will tell you the names of a given dog's parents, grandparents, great-grandparents, etc.

If you purchase a puppy whose sire and dam are not known but you believe it to be a purebred dog, you may apply to the AKC for an ILP number. An **I**ndefinite **L**isting **P**rivilege number allows you to exhibit the dog in AKC sporting events and earn titles. A dog with an ILP may not, however, be exhibited in the conformation ring or earn a breed Championship title.

To obtain an ILP number, write to the AKC for an application form. They will probably ask for pictures of your dog and written statements from knowledgable experts who testify that, in their opinions, your dog is purebred.

If, after investigating your claim, the AKC agrees that your dog is a purebred, they will issue a number and send you a certificate to that effect. From then on you may participate in AKC dog activities for fun.

PICKING A PUPPY

When choosing a German Shepherd puppy, take a hard look first at the environment. Is the atmosphere chaotic or orderly? Do the adult dogs appear friendly, healthy? Does the seller appear knowledgable about the breed? Is he concerned about the welfare of the

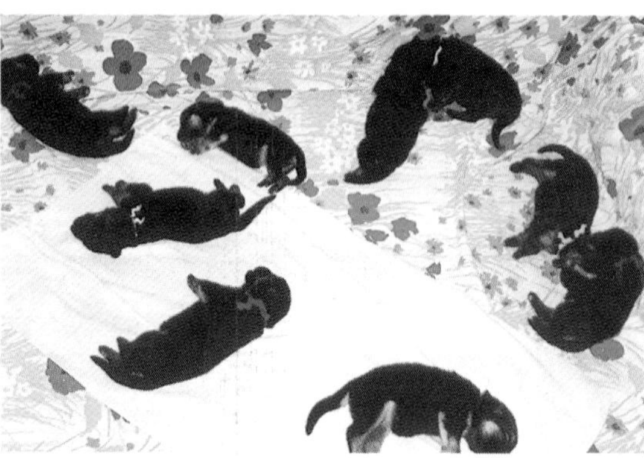

The colored collars on these 18-day-old pups help the breeder to identify them.

puppies and their future homes?

Next look at the whole litter and their living quarters. Their sleeping and play areas should be clean and free of unpleasant odors. If the puppies are using newspaper for elimination, it should be changed as needed. If they're outdoors, their elimination area should show signs of frequent clean-up.

Play fighting among littermates teaches combative skills as well as serving to develop muscles and coordination.

If possible, observe the puppies eating a meal and see how they react to each other. Look for puppies that eat eagerly and do not act aggressively toward littermates. Overprotectiveness of food at this early age may

This German Shepherd puppy has picked his new owner and doesn't want to let him go!

This pup has a very dark coat. The breeder will have a good idea of the puppy's eventual coat color as well as size and type.

signal problems in the adult dog.

Do the puppies appear active and healthy? They should have bright eyes with no discharge coming from them. Their stools should be well-formed with no signs of diarrhea. Their coats will be fluffy and full and should be clean and free of parasites, such as fleas and ticks.

As your eyes begin to focus on certain puppies in the litter, concentrate on their behavior for it often predicts what they will be like as adults. For example, the bully of the litter may grow up to become a very dominant individual sometimes difficult to control. The runt, or smallest one, may not fit your criteria for a busy lifestyle. He may grow up to be very timid or he may develop in the opposite direction and become the tyrant of the neighborhood.

A friendly, outgoing yet not hyperactive puppy begins life with a lot going for him. He should be curious and alert, show a bright intelligence in his expression, and be eager to hang around people.

Among dog folk there is an old saying that there are basically two kinds of dogs, dog-dogs and people-dogs. The dog-dogs are happiest when they're with their own kind and will spend their lives attempting to socialize with other dogs. Human companionship is secondary to them.

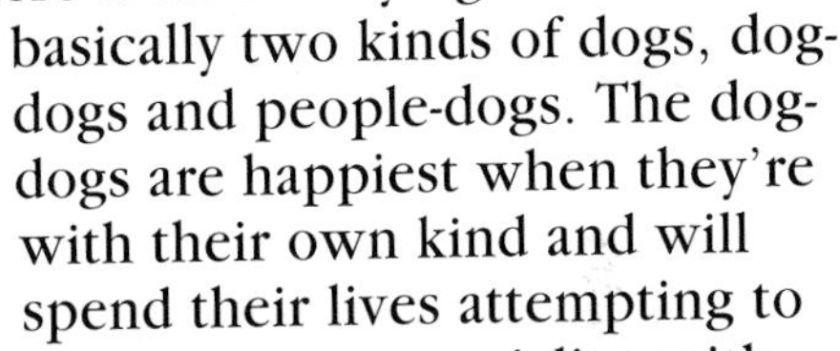

The puppy you choose should be curious and alert, showing intelligence in his expression.

People-dogs are more content to be with you. They accept other dogs, but prefer the company of their owners and will almost always choose you over other pets. This is the type of dog who will be eager to learn, anxious to please and happy doing things with you all his life.

If you're interested in exhibiting in the breed ring, not only must you consider temperament, but you must look at the puppy with an eye to what he'll look like as an adult. Here's where the help of the breeder is paramount. Nobody can accurately predict how a puppy will turn out, but the breeder, particularly if he has a history of raising good quality show dogs, is in a

When choosing a puppy, first take a look at the environment. It should be clean and free of unpleasant odors.

position to assist you in making the best choice. For example, the breeder will have a good idea of the puppy's eventual size, coat color and type.

The price of a show puppy will probably be a lot more than the price of a puppy destined for a pet home. After all the show dog will be shown at great cost in time, training and money, and ultimately bred to contribute more fine specimens to the breed in years to come. For example, if and when your puppy grows up to become a champion, the price you can demand for the stud fee of a male or the puppies of a female will be much higher than the price for puppies from pet stock.

On the other hand, you can purchase a pet-quality puppy out of the same litter from which a show-quality puppy comes. The difference in show and pet quality is often very small and noticeable only to trained experts.

The pet puppy, however, has come from the same parents, has had the same quality upbringing, and has received the same socialization and start in life that his show-quality littermate has had. The fact that the show puppy may have the potential for a thicker coat, a longer muzzle, or a heavier bone as an adult will not affect the pet-quality puppy or you. And you will be benefiting from the care and attention the entire litter received before, during and after birth.

In addition, you will still be able to train and exhibit your dog in obedience trials and earn titles for your dog. The sport of obedience is exciting and rewarding and is open to all purebred dogs regardless of whether or not they are show quality.

In fact, when you review your puppy's pedigree, you may see dogs listed with CD, CDX, UD, or UDX following their names. In German Shepherds particularly, these obedience titles are significant in demonstrating the willingness and capability of those individuals to work with their owners. To document this, the dogs have been exhibited at obedience trials thereby proving their value as companion animals.

As you begin to focus on certain puppies in the litter, concentrate on their behavior and how they interact with their littermates.

If the pedigree shows Sch. I, II, or III after the names of certain ancestors, this tells you that those dogs were tested and approved as protection dogs and have earned Schutzhund titles. Keep in mind that Schutzhund training demonstrates a dog's protectiveness, which is usually hereditary. Therefore, a smattering of protectiveness is fine, but a heavy dose of it may be more than you wish to live with in the adult dog.

If you're purchasing a puppy from a local hobby breeder who has bred a litter of puppies for the first time, you need to be particularly careful in your selection. First, the mother of the litter has no record of what she produces in size, coat color, temperament, etc. Ask the owner where the dam came from: that information could be a clue as to what you can expect from her puppies.

If the female was bred to a local pet male, you may want to visit his home and meet him. Study his behavior and observe his appearance and general physical condition as well as his disposition. If you don't like the parents, don't buy a puppy.

Perhaps, if you do your homework now, you may be as fortunate as I was many years ago when I purchased a female Miniature Schnauzer named Brandy from a first-time hobby breeder. Brandy's dam had been bred to a champion and the owner of the female was being guided in her breeding program by reputable breeders with years of experience.

The whole family, including children, should be involved in the selection of a new pet. This young girl carefully studies a litter of German Shepherd puppies.

Brandy ultimately grew up to be a fine specimen of the breed with a correct temperament. When she was two years old, I bred her to a champion and she produced four puppies. Two of them became champions and the start of a long line of well-known Miniature Schnauzers. Ask the owners of both parents about their pets' health. In particular, you will want to know whether or not either parent has a hereditary problem.

An adorable German Shepherd puppy patiently waits to be chosen by his new owner.

I said it before, and I will say it again. For the best chance at getting a German Shepherd Dog that will become a great companion, DO YOUR HOMEWORK!

If you do your homework, you will be successful in picking a fine German Shepherd that will grow into the dog you have always dreamed of!

CARING for Your German Shepherd Dog

The big day is about to arrive. You've done your homework, you've decided that a German Shepherd Dog is the best breed for you, you've found just the right puppy that makes your heart beat faster. What next? Before you introduce the new member of your family into your home, let's go over some of the things you'll need to think about and provide before you actually get the puppy. If you make appropriate arrangements now, you and the puppy will experience a smooth transition from birth environment to new home. The big day, even the weeks to come, will be smooth and pleasant for all concerned.

FEEDING

Talk to the seller and get a list of the kinds and brands of food the puppy has been fed. Dogs have very sensitive digestive systems so changing brands abruptly will usually cause diarrhea and great discomfort to the puppy to say nothing of the extra cleanup work for you.

Although your Shepherd may like chocolate, it can be very harmful to dogs. Its two basic chemicals, caffeine and theobromine, overstimulate the dog's nervous system.

Also record the number of meals per day that the puppy has been eating and the times of day he's eaten. Try to maintain this schedule for at least two weeks after you get him. Changing his environment and being separated from his dam and siblings is traumatic enough: he does not need physical stress added to this.

Dogs have very sensitive digestive systems and should not be fed human foods. A sip of water would surely be better to quench this Shepherd's thirst than a soft drink.

Water should also be available at all times during the day when he's out of his crate. At night, however, it's wise to restrict water consumption to a few sips after his last meal of the day. You and the puppy will not want to get up too many times during the night!

Never feed a puppy from your plate or the dinner table. It may be cute when he weighs ten pounds, but when he weighs 85 pounds and begs at the table, it won't be so much fun.

Dogs should eat dog food, not junk food. The major dog food manufacturers spend millions of dollars a year on researching the best diets for canines. Make use of this information and avoid feeding your puppy foods that will not help him grow properly or may cause stomach upset.

If and when you want to switch brands and/or types of dog food, talk to your veterinarian. He will suggest an appropriate diet and the amounts as well as number of meals per day that will most benefit your puppy.

As a general rule, puppies between two and six

An ideal snack for your German Shepherd is Chooz™. This is a hard molded bone of chicken and cheese that has a 70% protein content.

months of age should be served three meals a day. From six to 12 months, puppies should be given two meals a day. When the puppy reaches one year, you may feed him once or twice a day for life.

I prefer to feed my adults twice a day. That way, I can feed smaller amounts that will not cause stomach bloating and the dogs seem to enjoy eating at the same time as my family does. After all, smelling food cooking in the kitchen stimulates their appetites as well as ours, so twice daily works for us.

Always feed your puppy in the same place and never allow children to bother the puppy while he's eating. I choose to feed my dogs in the kitchen. It's clean, near the area of preparation, free of insects, which are attracted to bowls of food outdoors, and allows me an opportunity to observe how eagerly and how much each dog consumes.

Free feeding is an option whereby you place dry food in a bowl and just let the puppy help himself whenever the mood strikes. This method, however, has several disadvantages.

First, you'll never know exactly how much and when a puppy is eating. Secondly, food left out can spoil quickly in warm temperatures thereby making your dog sick. And thirdly, you miss seeing any subtle hints that the puppy is not feeling well when he nibbles half-heartedly.

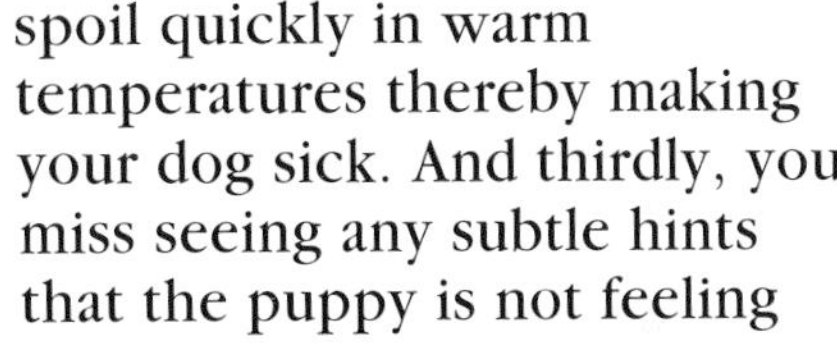

Stainless steel feeding bowls are the best for your dog, as they are durable and easy to clean.

By feeding on a regular schedule where you can observe the puppy eating, you're able to monitor the puppy's general health and exactly how he's feeling at any given time. Thus, when problems occur, this method draws your attention to the onset of trouble before it becomes serious.

When feeding puppies and adults, put down the food bowl and leave it alone for 15 minutes. At the end of that time, remove the bowl and offer no more food until the next scheduled meal. Dogs quickly figure out that when the food bowl is presented, they'd better get right to it before you take it away. No chance for attracting unwanted pests in the kitchen or for developing picky eaters this way, as well.

EXERCISE

There are several kinds of exercises we need to address. Exercising for elimination, for muscle building and coordination skills, for fun and bonding, and for learning are all important aspects of helping your puppy grow.

Elimination exercising should be limited to specific areas so the puppy learns that your command, "Let's go out!" (or whatever phrase you care to use) plus going to the same area each time will help him associate eliminating with your command. Taking him for long walks through the neighborhood is not the way to teach housetraining, as the puppy has so much to investigate that eliminating becomes lost in the adventure of exploring the neighborhood. Then, when he gets back in the house, he suddenly remembers he has to go and thereby another accident happens.

A game of fetch with a Gumbone® flying disc is good fun. Choose the disk with the bone on top.

Once the puppy is housebroken, he can be offered opportunities to discover his neighborhood. By then his body will also be strong enough to benefit from extended exercising.

Muscle building and coordination skills can be developed in the very young puppy with simple games of fetch played indoors. Since his bones are not fully grown and hardened, excessive exercising is dangerous and may cause physical problems later in life.

For the eight-week-old puppy, just

After a strenuous run in the brush, this German Shepherd cools off at the water's edge.

following you around the kitchen and family room will soon tire him out and he'll collapse into a deep sleep for anywhere from ten to 30 minutes. As the puppy grows, his capacity for exercise will increase and you'll see his need for more and more exercise grow with him.

If there are young children in the family, don't allow them to overdo play and exercise with the puppy. You should always be there to supervise any interaction between the children and the dog. Teaching children how to treat the puppy and teaching the puppy how to act with children is all part of your responsibility when raising them both.

One trick I developed years ago with children was to teach the "sit and hold" habit. Rather than let little children hold puppies when they were standing up, I taught the kids to sit on the floor when they wanted to hold a puppy. That way, if the puppy wriggled out of their arms, the puppy wouldn't have far to fall to the floor, thus preventing potentially serious accidents.

Taking the puppy to different environments such as a shopping center, park, beach, or a wooded trail not only serves to socialize the puppy but gives him plenty of exercise to strengthen his developing muscles. In addition, it serves to help you and the puppy build a strong bond of loyalty to each other.

Finally, exercising as a form of learning brings great pleasure to both teacher (you) and student (puppy). Playing hide-'n-seek in a fenced backyard is good exercise for the puppy while he learns to come to you for praise and a treat. Teaching the puppy to walk a "plank" builds his self-confidence while strengthening leg muscles as he walks along and tries not to fall off. (Use the bench seat of a picnic table or a narrow cement curb along a driveway. And always keep one hand on the puppy to prevent falls and assure him that all is well.)

Any active game that will encourage muscle development and be fun for the puppy is good exercise. Just remember not to play too much or for too long at any one time. Do not allow the puppy to jump until he's at least a year old, preferably 18 months to assure complete bone development. Puppies have short attention spans and even shorter muscle power endurance, so safety is an important criteria here.

Toys are an important part of puppy development for several reasons. First, every infant, whether human or animal, needs to learn to play because play is really practice for handling life situations when the infant becomes an adult. Make sure that the toys you provide are safe.

Play fighting, play hunting, play mating, play stalking, play grooming and power playing are nature's way of teaching the young puppy how to conduct himself

Taking your German Shepherd to different environments such as the beach not only serves to socialize your dog but also gives him plenty of room to exercise.

when he grows up. It provides practical lessons in how to interact with his own kind and succeed.

Play also provides an opportunity for muscle development. Running, chasing, catching, climbing and similar type activities are the means to teach the puppy how to use his own body to grow into a strong, physically skilled individual.

Secondly, playing with you is extremely beneficial to the bond you and the dog build together. Playing reinforces the idea that he is most certainly a vital member of your pack.

When you control the games–begin and end the games at your discretion, not the puppy's–it sends a further message to the puppy that you are the pack leader. That in itself teaches him to respect you, and makes his learning other behaviors more meaningful.

Finally, playing with other humans affords the puppy an opportunity to interact with people other than his leader. He learns to play gently with children and older people. He learns to inhibit his bite reflex and use his mouth in a gentle manner. He learns body control and how to use his energy efficiently. In other words, he learns self-control and the rewards it brings through attention and affection.

Outdoor pens allow dogs adequate space to exercise and breathe the fresh air. A cement or other hard-surface floor that allows for good drainage, easy cleaning and parasite-free space is recommended.

Suffice it to say that toys and playing are paramount to raising a well-rounded individual with good physical and mental skills that will serve him well for life.

Play fighting is a great way for your German Shepherd to expend energy. It also provides a practical lesson on how to interact with his own kind and succeed.

Grooming

Every dog needs to be groomed, even German Shepherds. Though they are not as demanding in their grooming needs as some terriers or Poodles, for example, their coats and skin will always need some attention.

Very young puppies have soft fluffy coats that give them that appealing cuddly appearance. As they grow, this soft coat begins to fall out and is replaced by two very different types of hair, a soft undercoat and a longer, stiffer type of hair that protects them from water and debris.

Proper brushing not only removes falling hair, it serves to stimulate the skin which, in turn, helps to develop that healthy, clean shine a good coat must have. Understanding the shedding process will enable you to prevent fur balls around the house and discomfort to your dog.

Unlike some short-coated breeds that shed constantly, German Shepherds exerpience two major shedding periods per year. During periods of heavy shedding, they should be brushed daily to remove dead hair and stimulate new growth.

At times of little or no shedding, the German Shepherd should be brushed every other day. Use a medium bristle brush and stroke with the lay of the hair. A metal dog comb is helpful in removing foreign matter. Stickers and burrs are often found under the neck and belly following a trek through fields and wild vegetation.

A hound glove used following a good brushing will bring up the natural oils in the skin and give the coat a healthy shine. Brushes, combs and gloves can be found in most pet shops and animal supply stores.

As for bathing your German Shepherd, this won't be necessary very often. A regular routine of brushing will keep his coat clean and looking good most of the time.

Dirt from mud is easy to remove. Simply allow the dirt to dry, then brush briskly and shine with the glove when you see that the coat is once again clean. Bathing too often dries the skin and hair and causes an unattractive dullness.

Many veterinarians and professional dog handlers suggest bathing no more than once every two to four weeks providing the dog is brushed daily. Dogs that live outdoors and run in the rain need bathing even less often.

Use a regular dog shampoo and warm water when you do bathe your Shepherd. Wet the dog down, apply shampoo and rub it into a lather the same way you shampoo your own hair. Rinse thoroughly with warm water and towel dry the dog immediately. Keep him out of drafts and cold air while he's drying or use a hair dryer on low heat to hasten the process. During cold weather, do not allow the dog to go outdoors until he's thoroughly dry.

If the dog gets paint or tar-type substances on his coat, apply a liberal

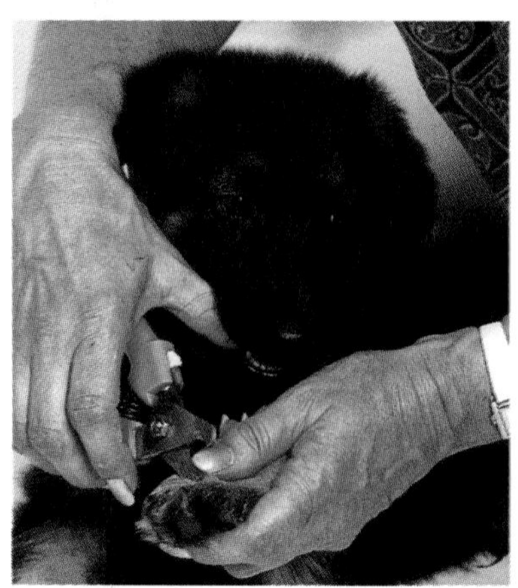

If you start trimming your puppy's nails at a young age and teach him to sit for this procedure, you'll have no problem when he is an adult.

amount of mineral oil to the paint, let it soak in for a few minutes, then rub briskly with an absorbent cloth. Follow with a good bath. Stronger chemicals used to remove paints can cause burning and irritation to the skin, which later may require veterinary attention.

A good brushing once the dog is dry will remove any dead hair not taken out by the bath. In addition, it will stimulate the release of those precious skin oils.

Two other matters of grooming must be mentioned here. Keeping your dog's teeth in good condition is essential for healthy gums. Your veterinarian will teach you how to clean your dog's teeth. He'll also suggest the best products to use for gum and teeth hygiene. There are a great variety of Nylabone® products available that veterinarians recommend as safe and healthy for your dog or puppy to chew on.

Grooming tools such as a comb, soft brush, slicker brush and shedding blade can be used to remove the dead hair from your German Shepherd's coat.

Toenails must be trimmed and this, too, can be learned from your veterinarian. If you start when your puppy is young and teach him to sit still for nail trimming, you'll have no problem when the puppy becomes an adult. However, some people wait until the dog is fully grown and by then the dog hates nail trimming so he threatens to bite the trimmer. This is unacceptable behavior.

At this point, the veterinarian will have to muzzle the dog for nail trimming and you'll have to pay for it. Make it economical for yourself and easy on the dog: teach nail trimming from an early age.

HOUSEBREAKING Your German Shepherd Dog

It must be noted that German Shepherds should not be trained to paper indoors because this will become an impossible situation when they are full grown. Success that comes by luck is usually a happenstance and frequently short-lived. Success that comes by well-thought-out, proven methods is often more easily achieved and permanent. This Success Method is designed to give you, the puppy owner, a simple yet proven way to help your puppy develop clean living habits and a feeling of security in his new environment.

TYPES OF TRAINING

You can train a puppy to relieve itself wherever you choose. For example, city dwellers often train their puppies to relieve themselves in the gutter because large plots of grass are not readily available. Suburbanites, on the other hand, usually have yards to accommodate their dogs' needs.

Outdoor training includes such surfaces as grass, dirt and cement. Indoor training usually means training a dog to newspaper or a paper-lined litter pan (appropriate for small and toy breeds).

When deciding on the surface and location that you'll want your dog to use, be sure it's going to be

Allow your dogs an opportunity to familiarize themselves with the area where they are to eliminate (and make sure to get out of the way!).

permanent. Training a dog to grass and then changing your mind two months later is extremely difficult for both the dog and the owner.

A whelping box can be lined with either newspaper or cotton sheets.

Next, choose the command you'll use each and every time you want your puppy to void. "Go hurry up," and "Go make," are examples of commands commonly used by dog owners.

Get in the habit of asking the puppy, "Do you want to go hurry up?" (or whatever your chosen relief command is) before you take him out. That way, when he becomes an adult, you'll be able to determine if he wants to go out when you ask him. A confirmation will be signs of interest,

Once the puppies are moved out of the whelping box, their area should be lined with the same material that was in the whelping box. This will make housebreaking easier.

A grown Shepherd (or two) on a bed doesn't leave much room for the human occupant! When you first get your puppy, you should decide if he'll be allowed on your bed when he is an adult.

wagging his tail, watching you intently, going to the door, etc.

Most of all, be consistent. Always take your dog to the same location, always use the same command, and always have him on lead when he's in his relief area.

By following the Success Method, your puppy will be completely house-trained by the time his muscle and brain development reach maturity. Keep in mind that small breeds usually mature faster than large breeds, but all puppies should be trained by six months of age.

Puppy's Needs

A puppy needs to relieve himself after play periods, after each meal, after he's been sleeping and any time he indicates he's looking for a place to urinate or defecate.

The urinary and intestinal tract muscles of very young puppies are not fully developed. Therefore, like human babies, puppies need to relieve themselves frequently.

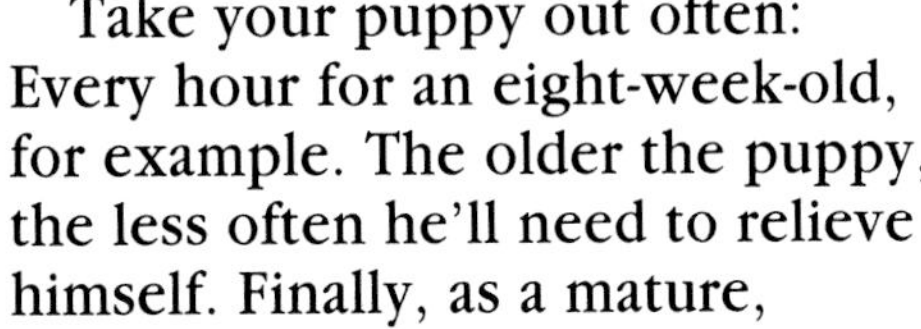

Provide a soft bed for your dog. A bean bag dog bed is big enough for two!

Take your puppy out often: Every hour for an eight-week-old, for example. The older the puppy, the less often he'll need to relieve himself. Finally, as a mature, healthy adult, he'll require only three to five relief trips per day.

Housing

Since the type of housing and control you provide for your puppy has a direct relationship on the success of housetraining, we consider the various aspects of both before we begin training.

Bringing a new puppy home and turning him loose in your house can be compared to turning a child loose in a sports arena and telling the child the place is all his! The sheer enormity of the place would be too much for him to handle.

Instead, offer the puppy clearly defined areas where he can play, sleep, eat and live. A room of the house where the family gathers the most is the obvious choice. Puppies are social animals and need to feel a part of the pack right from the start. Hearing your voice, watching you while you're doing things, smelling you nearby are all positive reinforcers that he is now a member of your pack. Usually a family room, the kitchen or a nearby adjoining breakfast nook is ideal for providing safety and security for both puppy and owner.

Within that room, there should be a smaller area that the puppy can call his own. A cubby hole, a wire or fiberglass dog crate, or a fenced (not boarded!) corner from which he can view the activities of his new family will be fine.

The size of the area or crate is the key factor here. The area must be large enough for the puppy to lay down and stretch out as well as stand up without rubbing his head on the top, yet small enough so that he cannot relieve himself at one end and sleep at the other without coming into contact with his droppings.

Dogs are, by nature, clean animals and will not remain close to their relief areas unless forced to do so. In those cases, they then become dirty dogs and usually remain that way for life.

The most important thing to remember when training your German Shepherd puppy is to always praise the puppy lavishly whenever he does something right.

By providing sleeping and resting quarters that fit the dog, and offering frequent opportunities to relieve himself outside his quarters, the puppy quickly learns that the outdoors is the place to go when he needs to urinate or defecate. It also reinforces his innate desire to keep his sleeping quarters clean. This, in turn, helps develop the control muscles that will eventually produce a dog with clean living habits.

The crate or cubby should be lined with a clean towel and offer one toy, no more. Do not put food or water in the crate as eating and drinking will activate his digestive processes and ultimately defeat your purpose as well as make the puppy very uncomfortable as he attempts to "hold it."

Never line his sleeping area with newspaper. Puppy litters are usually raised on newspaper and, once in your home, the puppy will immediately associate newspaper with voiding. Never put newspaper on any

floor while housetraining as this will only confuse the puppy. Finally, restrict water intake after evening meals. Offer a few licks at a time: Never let a young puppy gulp water after meals.

In addition to his crate, you may want to provide a soft bed for your puppy that he can use at will whenever he's in the house yet not in his crate. A bean bag bed is ideal for this purpose. Oval wicker baskets are nice, but offer too much opportunity for destructive chewing. The soft wicker sides are usually right at the level of the dog's mouth.

When he's in his soft bed, perhaps chewing on a toy, you must supervise him and take the bed away if he decides to use the bed itself as a chew toy. Waiting until he's completed the teething process will assure that he doesn't develop bad habits of chewing on furniture.

Save his soft bed for later months and years. (I recall that one of my Shepherds, Morgan, was two years old before I could give him a bean bag that he didn't try to chew up! However, once he reached maturity, he used that bed for the rest of his life.)

CONTROL

By control we mean helping the puppy to create a lifestyle pattern that will be compatible to that of his human pack (You!). Just as we guide little children to learn our way of life, we must show the puppy when it's time to play, eat, sleep, exercise, even entertain himself.

Your puppy should always sleep in his crate. He should also learn that, during times of household confusion and excessive

For a puppy exercise can consist of a short walk around the yard.

human activity, such as at breakfast when family members are preparing for the day, he can play by himself in relative safety and comfort in his crate. Each time you leave the puppy alone, he should be crated. Puppies are chewers. They can't tell the difference between lamp cords, television wires, shoes, table legs, etc. Chewing into a television wire, for example, can be fatal to the puppy while a shorted wire can start a fire in the house.

Young puppies need to eliminate upon awakening from naps. If kept in an outdoor pen such as this one, there should be a separate area for elimination that is cleaned regularly.

If the puppy chews on the arm of a chair when he's alone, you will probably discipline him angrily when you get home. Thus, he makes the association that your coming home means he's going to be hit or punished. (He won't remember chewing up the chair and is incapable of making the association of the discipline with the naughty deed.)

If you have a small child in the home who wants to get into the puppy's food bowl every time he eats, feeding the pup in his crate is the answer. The child can't disturb the dog, and the pup will be free to eat in peace.

Other times of excitement, such as family parties, etc., can be fun for the puppy providing he can view the activities from the security of his crate. He's not underfoot, he's not being fed all sorts of tidbits which will probably cause him stomach distress, yet he still feels a part of the fun.

SCHEDULE

As stated earlier, a puppy should be taken to his relief area each time he's released from his crate, after meals, after each play session, when he first awakens in the morning (at age eight weeks, this can mean 5 AM!), and whenever he indicates by circling or sniffing busily that he needs to urinate or defecate. For puppies under ten weeks of age, a routine of taking him out every hour is necessary. As the puppy grows, he'll be able to wait for longer periods of time.

Keep trips to his relief area short. Stay no more than five or six minutes and then return to the house. If he goes during that time, praise lavishly and take him indoors immediately. If he doesn't, but he has an accident when you go back indoors, pick him up immediately, say, "No! No!" and return to the house again. NEVER hit a puppy or rub his face in urine or excrement when he has an accident.

Once indoors, put him in his crate until you've had time to clean up his accident. Then release him to the family area and watch him more closely then before. Chances are, his accident was a result of your not picking up his signal or waiting too long before offering him the opportunity to relieve himself. NEVER hold a grudge against the puppy for accidents.

A puppy should also have regular play and exercise sessions when he's with you or your family members. Exercise for a very young puppy can consist of a short walk around the house or yard. Playing can include fetching games with a ball, such as a Gumaball®: these balls are made of polyurethane–they bounce and are soft. (All puppies teethe and need soft things on which to chew.) Remember to restrict play periods to indoors within his living area (the family room, for example) until he's completely housetrained.

Let the puppy learn that going outdoors means it's time to relieve himself, not play. Once trained, he'll be able to play indoors and out and still differentiate the times for play versus the times for relief.

Help him develop regular hours for naps, being alone, playing by himself and just resting, all in his crate. Encourage him to entertain himself while you're busy with your activities. Let him learn that having you near is comforting, but your main purpose in life is not to provide him with undivided attention.

Playing can include fetching games with a Gumaball®. These balls are made of polyurethane and are softer than nylon.

At the age of nine weeks this young German Shepherd already wears a simple buckle collar, which will make him much easier to control during training periods.

Each time you put the puppy in his crate, tell him "It's cubby time" (or whatever command you choose). Soon, he'll run to his crate when he hears you say

A well-trained German Shepherd can be taught to go to the door when he needs to go out.

those words.

In the beginning of his training, don't leave him in his crate for prolonged periods of time except during the night when everyone is sleeping. Make his experience with his crate a pleasant one and, as an adult, he'll love it and willingly stay in it for several hours. (There are millions of people who go to work every day and leave their adult dogs crated while they're away. The dogs accept this as their lifestyle and look forward to "crate time.")

Crate training provides safety for you, the puppy and the home. It also provides the puppy with a feeling of security, and that helps develop a puppy with self-confidence and clean habits.

Six Steps to Successful Training

Remember, one of the primary ingredients in housetraining your puppy is control. And regardless of your lifestyle, there will always be occasions when you'll need to have a place where your dog can stay and be happy and safe. Crate training is the answer for now and in the future.

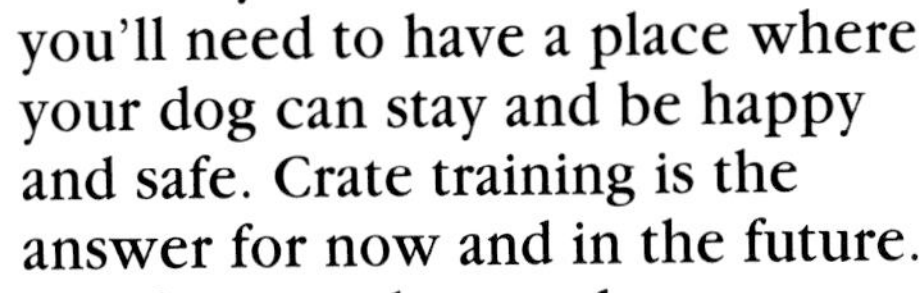

Below are the step-by-step directions to actually training your puppy to accept his crate as his den, a place of security and comfort. Follow each step in order and don't try to rush the final steps. A conscientious approach to training now will result in a happy dog that willingly accepts your lifestyle as his own.

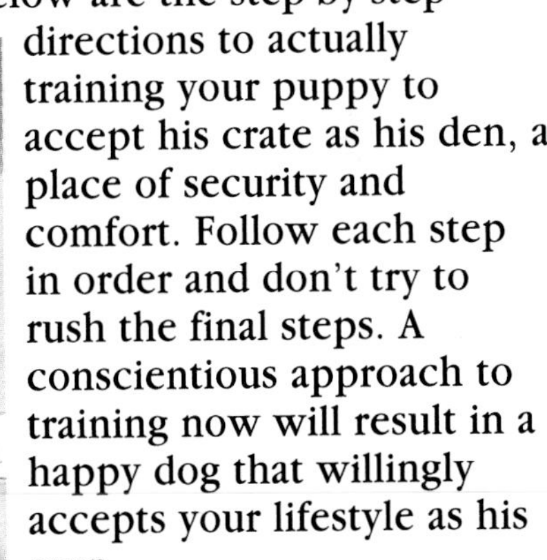

Your puppy should become accustomed to wearing a collar at a young age—the sooner the better.

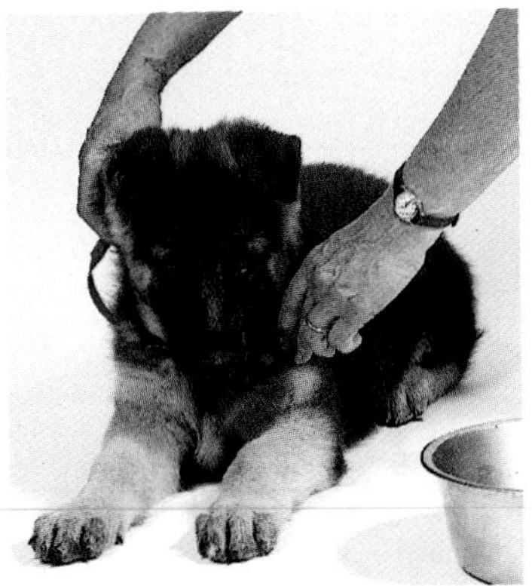

1. Tell the puppy, "It's cubby time!" and place him in the crate with a small treat (a piece of cheese or half a biscuit). Let him stay in the crate for five or ten minutes while you are in the same room. Then release him and praise lavishly. Never release him when he's fussing. Wait until he's quiet before you let him out.
2. Repeat Step 1 several times a day.
3. The next day, place the puppy in the crate as before. Let him stay there for ten minutes. Do this several times.
4. Continue building time in five-minute increments until the puppy will stay in his crate for 30 minutes with you in the room. Always take him to his relief

area after prolonged periods in his crate.

5. Now go back to the beginning and let puppy stay in his crate for five minutes while you are *out* of the room.
6. Once again build crate time in five minute increments with you out of the room. When puppy will stay willingly in his crate (he may even fall asleep!) for 30 minutes with you out of the room, he'll be ready to stay in it for several hours at a time.

A few key elements are really all you need to a successful house and crate training method: consistency, frequency, praise, control and supervision. By following this Sucess Method with a normal, healthy puppy, you and the puppy will soon be past the stage of "accidents" and ready to move on to a full and rewarding life together.

One of the most important things you must teach your puppy is to come when you call him. This command could save his life one day.

CANINE DEVELOPMENT SCHEDULE

First through third period–Birth through seven weeks.

Puppy needs food, sleep, warmth and responds to simple and gentle touching. Needs mother for security and disciplining. Needs littermates for learning interaction with other dogs. Pup learns to function within a pack and learns pack order of dominance. Begin socializing with adults and children for short periods. Begins to become aware of its environment.

Fourth period–Eight through 12 weeks.

Brain is fully developed. Needs socializing with outside world. Remove from mother and littermates. Needs to change from canine pack to human pack. Human dominance necessary. Fear period occurs between eight and 16 weeks. Avoid fright and pain.

Fifth period–13 through 16 weeks.

Training and formal obedience should begin. Less

association with other dogs, more with people, places, situations. Period will pass easily if you remember this is pup's change-to-adolescence time. Be firm and fair. Flight instinct prominent. Permissiveness and over-disciplining can do permanent damage. Praise for good behavior.

Juvenile period–Four months through eight months.

Another fear period about seven to eight months of age. It passes quickly, but be cautious of fright and pain. Sexual maturity reached. Dominant traits established. Dog should understand sit, down, come and stay by now.

Note–These are approximate time frames. Allow for individual differences in puppies.

OBEDIENCE TRAINING

Finally make plans to take your puppy to a training class. Kindergarten classes are for puppies from eight to 20 weeks of age while beginner's obedience classes are for puppies over five months of age.

Training your Shepherd is essential to your own happiness as well as the dog's. Young puppies need to be taught good manners, what is and is not

Obedience training classes are offered in most areas. Dog trainer Max Lee and a German Shepherd demonstrate heeling at an obedience class in Malaysia.

acceptable behavior, and that you are the pack leader and must be respected as such. With no clue as to the hierarchy of his pack and no idea of his own physical strength, an untrained German Shepherd is always a risk. So train your puppy right from the start.

Anticipating your puppy's needs, satisfying his desires, and sharing life's wonders with him can be the most rewarding experience you'll ever have. Enjoy it all, especially enjoy living with and loving a German Shepherd Dog. He'll make all your efforts worthwhile.

In an obedience class you will learn how to teach your dog to walk beside you without pulling. This is known as the heel exercise.

Young German Shepherds need to be taught good manners, what is and is not acceptable behavior, and to respect their owner as the pack leader.

SPORT of Purebred Dogs

Welcome to the exciting and sometimes frustrating sport of dogs. No doubt you are trying to learn more about dogs or you wouldn't be deep into this book. This section covers the basics that may entice you, further your knowledge and help you to understand the dog world. If you decide to give showing, obedience or any other dog activities a try, then I suggest you seek further help from the appropriate source.

Dog showing has been a very popular sport for a long time and has been taken quite seriously by some. Others only enjoy it as a hobby.

Aside from the dazzling trophies it awards, dog showing is rewarding in many ways for both owner and dog.

The Kennel Club in England was formed in 1859, the American Kennel Club was established in 1884 and the Canadian Kennel Club was formed in 1888. The purpose of these clubs was to register purebred dogs and maintain their Stud Books. In the beginning, the concept of registering dogs was not readily accepted. More than 36 million dogs have been enrolled in the AKC Stud Book since its inception in 1888. Presently the kennel clubs not only register dogs but adopt and enforce rules and regulations governing dog shows, obedience trials and field trials. Over the years they have fostered and encouraged interest in the health and welfare of the purebred dog. They routinely donate funds to veterinary research for study on genetic disorders.

Listed are the addresses of the kennel clubs in the United States, Great Britain and Canada.

Conformation showing is based on the dog's appearance–that is his structure, movement and attitude. Here a judge carefully examines a German Shepherd.

The American Kennel Club
51 Madison Avenue
New York, NY 10010
(Their registry is located at: 5580 Centerview Drive, STE 200, Raleigh, NC 27606-3390)

The Kennel Club
1 Clarges Street
Piccadilly, London, WIY 8AB, England

The Canadian Kennel Club
111 Eglinton Avenue
East Toronto, Ontario M6S 4V7
Canada

Today there are numerous activities that are enjoyable for both the dog and the handler. Some of the activities include conformation showing, obedience competition, tracking, agility, the Canine Good Citizen Certificate, and a wide range of instinct tests that vary from breed to breed. Where you start depends upon your goals which early on may not be readily apparent.

CONFORMATION

Conformation showing is our oldest dog show sport. This type of showing is based on the dog's appearance–that is his structure, movement and attitude. When considering this type of showing, you need to be aware of your breed's standard and be able to evaluate your dog compared to that standard. The breeder of your puppy or other experienced breeders would be good sources for such an evaluation. Puppies can go through lots of changes over a period of time. I always say most puppies start out as promising and then after maturing may be disappointing as show candidates. Even so this should not deter them from being excellent pets.

German Shepherds are popular show dogs and there are often many in every class. Earning a championship can be very challenging.

Usually conformation training classes are offered by the local kennel or obedience clubs. These are excellent places for training puppies. The puppy should be able to walk on a lead before entering such a class. Proper ring procedure and technique for posing (stacking) the dog will be demonstrated as well as gaiting the dog. Usually certain patterns are used in the ring such as the triangle or the "L." Conformation class, like the PKT class, will give your youngster the opportunity to socialize with different breeds of dogs and humans too.

It takes some time to learn the routine of conformation showing. Usually one starts at the puppy matches which may be AKC Sanctioned or Fun Matches. These matches are generally for puppies from two or three months to a year old, and there may be classes for the adult over the age of 12 months. Similar to point shows, the classes are divided by sex and after completion of the classes in that breed or variety, the class winners compete for Best of Breed or Variety. The winner goes on to compete in the Group and the Group winners compete for Best in Match. No championship points are awarded for match wins.

A German Shepherd meets another dog in an AKC Canine Good Citizen test. This program was designed to encourage owners to train their dogs.

A few matches can be great training for puppies even though there is no intention to go on showing. Matches enable the puppy to meet new people and be handled by a stranger–the judge. It is also a change of environment, which broadens the horizon for both dog and handler. Matches and other dog activities boost the confidence of the handler and especially the younger handlers.

Earning an AKC championship is built on a point system, which is different from Great Britain. To become an AKC Champion of Record the dog must earn 15 points. The number of points earned each time depends upon the number of dogs in competition. The number of points available at each show depends upon the breed, its sex and the location of the show. The United States is divided into ten AKC zones. Each zone has its own set of points. The purpose of the zones is to try to equalize the points available from breed to breed and area to area. The AKC adjusts the point scale annually.

The number of points that can be won at a show are between one and five. Three-, four- and five-point wins are considered majors. Not only does the dog need 15 points won under three different judges, but those points must include two majors under two different judges. Canada also works on a point system but majors are not required.

Junior Showmanship

The Junior Showmanship Class is a wonderful way to build self confidence even if there are no aspirations of staying with the dog-show game later in life. Frequently, Junior Showmanship becomes the background of those who become successful exhibitors/handlers in the future. In some instances it is taken very seriously, and success is measured in terms of wins. The Junior Handler is judged solely on his ability and skill in presenting his dog. The dog's conformation is not to be considered by the judge. Even so the condition and grooming of the dog may be a reflection upon the handler.

CANINE GOOD CITIZEN

The AKC sponsors a program to encourage dog owners to train their dogs. Local clubs perform the pass/fail tests, and dogs who pass are awarded a Canine Good Citizen Certificate. Proof of vaccination is required at the time of participation. The test includes:

1. Accepting a friendly stranger.
2. Sitting politely for petting.
3. Appearance and grooming.
4. Walking on a loose leash.
5. Walking through a crowd.
6. Sit and down on command/staying in place.

7. Come when called.
8. Reaction to another dog.
9. Reactions to distractions.
10. Supervised separation.

If more effort was made by pet owners to accomplish these exercises, fewer dogs would be cast off to the humane shelter.

German Shepherds excel at tracking. This dog pulls hard on the tracking line to tell his owner, "The track goes this way."

Obedience

Obedience is necessary, without a doubt, but it can also become a wonderful hobby or even an obsession. In my opinion, obedience classes and competition can provide wonderful companionship, not only with your dog but with your classmates or fellow competitors. It is always gratifying to discuss your dog's problems with others who have had similar experiences. The AKC acknowledged Obedience

German Shepherd brace, or pair, doing figure 8 heeling in Obedience trial.

around 1936, and it has changed tremendously even though many of the exercises are basically the same. Today, obedience competition is just that–very competitive. Even so, it is possible for every obedience exhibitor to come home a winner (by earning qualifying scores) even though he/she may not earn a placement in the class.

TRACKING

Tracking is officially classified obedience, but I feel it should have its own category. There are three tracking titles available: Tracking Dog (TD), Tracking Dog Excellent (TDX), Variable Surface Tracking (VST). If all three tracking titles are obtained, then the dog officially becomes a CT (Champion Tracker). The CT will go in front of the dog's name.

A TD may be earned anytime and does not have to follow the other obedience titles. There are many exhibitors that prefer tracking to obedience, and there are others like myself that do both. In my experience with small dogs, I prefer to earn the CD and CDX before attempting tracking. My reasoning is that small dogs are closer to the mat in the obedience rings and therefore it's too easy to put the nose down and sniff. Tracking encourages sniffing. Of course this depends on the dog. I've had some dogs that tracked around the ring and others (TDXs) who wouldn't think of sniffing in the ring.

AGILITY

Agility was first introduced by John Varley in England at the Crufts Dog Show, February 1978, but Peter Meanwell, competitor and judge, actually developed the idea. It was

Agility is a fascinating sport that the dog, handler and spectators enjoy. This German Shepherd is being led over the teeter-totter obstacle.

officially recognized in the early '80s. Agility is extremely popular in England and Canada and growing in popularity in the U.S. The AKC acknowledged agility in August 1994. Dogs must be at least 12 months of age to be entered. It is a fascinating sport that the dog, handler and spectators enjoy to the utmost. Agility is a spectator sport! The dog performs off lead. The handler either runs with his dog or positions himself on the course and directs his dog with verbal and hand signals over a timed course over or through a variety of obstacles including a time out or pause. One of the main drawbacks to agility is finding a place to train. The obstacles take up a lot of space and it is very time consuming to put up and take down courses.

Schutzhund was originally a test to determine which German Shepherds were quality dogs for breeding. Today it is a fast growing competitive sport to test dogs for correct temperament and working ability.

Schutzhund

The German word "Schutzhund" translated to English means "Protection Dog." It is a fast growing competitive sport in the United States and has been popular in England since the early 1900s. Schutzhund was originally a test to determine which German Shepherds were quality dogs for breeding in Germany. It gives us the ability to test our dogs for correct temperament and working ability. Like every other dog sport, it requires teamwork between the handler and the dog.

Schutzhund training and showing involves three phases: Tracking, Obedience and Protection. There are three SchH levels: SchH I (novice), SchH II (intermediate), and SchH III (advanced). Each title becomes progressively more difficult. The handler and dog start out in each phase with 100 points. Points are deducted as errors are incurred. A total perfect score is 300, and for a dog and handler to earn a title he must earn at least 70 points in tracking and obedience and at least 80 points in protection. Today many different breeds participate successfully in Schutzhund.

TRAVELING with Your Dog

The earlier you start traveling with your new puppy or dog, the better. He needs to become accustomed to traveling. However, some dogs are nervous riders and become carsick easily. It is helpful if he starts with an empty stomach. Do not despair, as it will go better if you continue taking him with you on short fun rides. How would you feel if every time you rode in the car you stopped at the doctor's for an injection? You would soon dread that nasty car. Older dogs that tend to get carsick may have more of a problem adjusting to traveling. Those dogs that are having a serious problem may benefit from some medication prescribed by the veterinarian.

Do give your dog a chance to relieve himself before getting into the car. It is a good idea to be prepared for a clean up with a leash, paper towels, bag and terry cloth towel.

The safest place for your dog is in a fiberglass crate, although close confinement can promote carsickness in some dogs. If your dog is nervous you can try letting him ride on the seat next to you or in someone's lap.

An alternative to the crate would be to use a car harness made for dogs and/or a safety strap attached to the harness or collar. Whatever you do, do not let your dog ride in the back of a pickup truck unless he is securely tied on a very short lead. I've seen trucks stop quickly and, even though the dog was tied, it fell out and was dragged.

Never let your dogs stick their heads out of an open window while the car is moving, as foreign debris can blow into their eyes.

I do occasionally let my dogs ride loose with me because I really enjoy their companionship, but in all honesty they are safer in their crates. I have a friend whose van rolled in an accident but his dogs, in their fiberglass crates, were not injured nor did they escape. Another advantage of the crate is that it is a safe place to leave him if you need to run into the store. Otherwise you wouldn't be able to leave the windows down. Keep in mind that while many dogs are overly protective in their crates, this may not be enough to deter dognappers. In some states it is against the law to leave a dog in the car unattended.

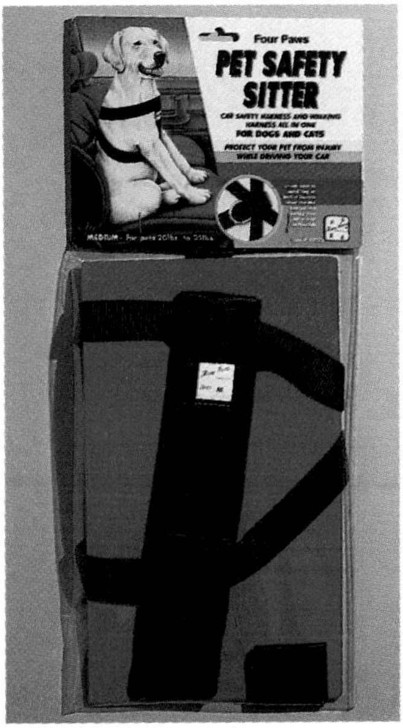

The Pet Safety Sitter is designed to protect dogs from injury by securing them in place and preventing them from disturbing drivers and passengers. Photo courtesy of Four Paws.

Never leave a dog loose in the car wearing a collar and leash. I have known more than one dog that has killed himself by hanging. Do not let him put his head out an open window. Foreign debris can be blown into his eyes. When leaving your dog unattended in a car, consider the temperature. It can take less than five minutes to reach temperatures over 100 degrees F.

Trips

Perhaps you are taking a trip. Give consideration to what is best for your dog–traveling with you or boarding. When traveling by car, van or motor home, you need to think ahead about locking your vehicle. In all probability you have many valuables in the car and do not wish to leave it unlocked. Perhaps most valuable and not replaceable is your dog. Give thought to securing your vehicle and providing adequate ventilation for him, it's best not to leave him at all. Another consideration for you when traveling with your dog is medical problems that may arise and little inconveniences, such as exposure to external parasites. Some areas of the country are quite flea infested. You may want to carry flea spray with you. This is even a good idea when staying in motels. Quite possibly you are not the only occupant of the room.

Unbelievably many motels and even hotels do allow canine guests, even some very first-class ones. Gaines Pet Foods Corporation publishes *Touring With Towser*, a directory of domestic hotels and motels that accommodate guests with dogs. Their address is Gaines TWT, PO Box 5700, Kankakee, IL, 60902. I would recommend you call ahead to any motel that you may be considering and see if they accept pets. Sometimes it is necessary to pay a deposit against room damage. Of course you are more likely to gain accommodations for a small dog than a large dog. Also the management feels reassured when you mention that your dog will be crated. Since my dogs tend to bark when I leave the room, I leave the TV on nearly full blast to deaden the noises outside that tend to encourage my dogs to bark. If you do travel with your dog, take along plenty of baggies so that you can clean up after him. When we all do our share in cleaning up, we make it possible for motels to continue accepting our pets. As a matter of fact, you should practice cleaning up everywhere you take your dog.

Depending on where your are traveling, you may need an up-to-date health certificate issued by your veterinarian. It is good policy to take along your dog's medical information, which would include the name, address and phone number of your veterinarian, vaccination record, rabies certificate, and any medication he is taking.

AIR TRAVEL

When traveling by air, you need to contact the airlines to check their policy. Usually you have to make arrangements up to a couple of weeks in advance for traveling with your dog. The airlines require your dog to travel in an airline approved fiberglass crate. Usually these can be purchased through the airlines but they are also readily available in most pet-supply stores. If your dog is not accustomed to a crate, then it is a good idea to get him acclimated to it before your trip. The day of the actual trip you should withhold water about one hour ahead of departure and no food for about 12 hours. The airlines generally have temperature restrictions, which do not allow pets to travel if it is either too cold or too hot. Frequently these restrictions are based on the temperatures at the departure and arrival airports. It's best to inquire about a health certificate. These usually need to be issued within ten days of departure. You should arrange for non-stop, direct flights and if a commuter plane should be involved, check to see if it will carry dogs. Some don't. The Humane Society of the United States has put together a tip sheet for airline traveling. You can receive a copy by sending a self-addressed stamped envelope to:

The Humane Society of the United States
Tip Sheet
2100 L Street NW
Washington, DC 20037.

Regulations differ for

Crates are a safe way for your dog to travel. The fiberglass crates are safest but the metal crates allow more air.

traveling outside of the country and are sometimes changed without notice. Well in advance you need to write or call the appropriate consulate or agricultural department for instructions. Some countries have lengthy quarantines (six months), and countries differ in their rabies vaccination requirements. For instance, it may have to be given at least 30 days ahead of your departure.

A fiberglass travel crate such as this one is required for airline travel. It is a good idea to acclimate your dog to the traveling crate before you go.

Do make sure your dog is wearing proper identification. You never know when you might be in an accident and separated from your dog. Or your dog could be frightened and somehow manage to escape and run away. When I travel, my dogs wear collars with engraved nameplates with my name, phone number and city.

Another suggestion would be to carry in-case-of-emergency instructions. These would include the address and phone number of a relative or friend, your veterinarian's name, address and phone number, and your dog's medical information.

BOARDING KENNELS

Perhaps you have decided that you need to board your dog. Your veterinarian can recommend a good boarding facility or possibly a pet sitter that will come to your house. It is customary for the boarding kennel to ask for proof of vaccination for the DHLPP, rabies and bordetella vaccine. The bordetella should have been given within six months of boarding. This is for your protection. If they do not ask for this proof I would not

If you decide that you need to board your dog, your veterinarian can recommend a reputable boarding facility.

board at their kennel. Ask about flea control. Those dogs that suffer flea-bite allergy can get in trouble at a boarding kennel. Unfortunately boarding kennels are limited on how much they are able to do.

For more information on pet sitting, contact NAPPS:
National Association of Professional Pet Sitters
1200 G Street, NW
Suite 760
Washington, DC 20005.

Our clinic has technicians that pet sit and technicians that board clinic patients in their homes. This may be an alternative for you. Ask your veterinarian if they have an employee that can help you. There is a definite advantage of having a technician care for your dog, especially if your dog is on medication or is a senior citizen.

You can write for a copy of *Traveling With Your Pet* from ASPCA, Education Department, 441 E. 92nd Street, New York, NY 10128.

DENTAL CARE for Your Dog's Life

So you've got a new puppy! You also have a new set of puppy teeth in your household. Anyone who has ever raised a puppy is abundantly aware of these new teeth. Your puppy will chew anything it can reach, chase your shoelaces, and play "tear the rag" with any piece of clothing it can find. When puppies are newly born, they have no teeth. At about four weeks of age, puppies of most breeds begin to develop their deciduous or baby teeth. They begin eating semi-solid food, fighting and biting with their litter mates, and learning discipline from their mother. As their new teeth come in, they inflict more pain on their mother's breasts, so her feeding sessions become less frequent and shorter. By six or eight weeks, the mother will start growling to warn her pups when they are fighting too roughly or hurting her as they nurse too much with their new teeth.

Nylafloss® is a nylon tug toy that is actually dental floss. Do not use cotton tug toys as cotton is weak and easily loses strands, which are indigestible should the dog swallow them.

Puppies need to chew. It is a necessary part of their physical and mental development. They develop muscles and necessary life skills as they drag objects around, fight over possession, and vocalize alerts and warnings. Puppies chew on things to explore their world. They are using their sense of taste to determine what is food and what is not. How else can they tell an electrical cord from a lizard? At about four months of age, most puppies begin shedding their baby teeth. Often these teeth need some help to come out and make way for the permanent teeth. The incisors (front teeth) will be replaced first. Then, the adult canine or fang teeth erupt. When the baby tooth is not shed before the permanent tooth comes in, veterinarians call it a retained deciduous tooth. This condition will often cause gum infections by trapping hair and debris between the permanent tooth and the retained baby tooth. Nylafloss® is an excellent device for puppies to use. They can toss it, drag it, and chew on the many surfaces it presents. The baby teeth can catch in the nylon material, aiding in their removal. Puppies that have adequate chew toys will have less destructive behavior, develop more physically, and have less chance of retained deciduous teeth.

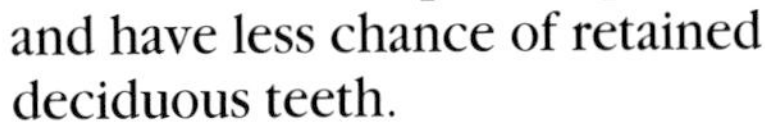

During the first year, your dog should be seen by your veterinarian at regular intervals. Your veterinarian will let you know when to bring in your puppy for vaccinations and parasite examinations. At each visit, your veterinarian should inspect the lips, teeth, and mouth as part of a complete physical examination. You should take some part in the maintenance of your dog's oral health. You should examine your dog's mouth weekly throughout his first year to make sure there are no sores, foreign objects, tooth problems, etc. If your dog drools excessively, shakes its head, or has bad breath, consult your veterinarian. By the time your dog is six months old, the permanent teeth are all in and plaque can start to accumulate on the tooth surfaces. This is when your dog needs to develop good dental-care habits to prevent calculus build-up on its teeth. Brushing is best. That is a fact that cannot be denied. However, some dogs do not like their teeth brushed regularly, or you may not be able to accomplish the task. In that case, you should consider a product that will help prevent plaque and calculus build-up.

The entertainment value of Gumabone® products is but an added advantage to the fighting of tooth decay and periodontitis.

The Plaque Attackers® and Galileo Bone® are other excellent

choices for the first three years of a dog's life. Their shapes make them interesting for the dog. As the dog chews on them, the solid polyurethane massages the gums which improves the blood circulation to the periodontal tissues. Projections on the chew devices increase the surface and are in contact with the tooth for more efficient cleaning. The unique shape and consistency prevent your dog from exerting excessive force on his own teeth or from breaking off pieces of the bone. If your dog is an aggressive chewer or weighs more than 55 pounds (25 kg), you should consider giving him a Nylabone®, the most durable chew product on the market.

The Gumabone®, made by the Nylabone Company, is constructed of strong polyurethane, which is softer than nylon. Less powerful chewers prefer the Gumabones® to the Nylabones®. A super option for your dog is the Hercules Bone®, a uniquely shaped bone named after the great Olympian for its exceptional strength. Like all Nylabone products, they are specially scented to make them attractive to your dog. Ask your veterinarian about these bones and he will validate the good doctor's prescription: Nylabones® not only give your dog a good chewing workout but also help to save your dog's teeth (and even his life, as it protects him from possible fatal periodontal diseases).

By the time dogs are four years old, 75% of them have periodontal disease. It is the most common infection in dogs. Yearly examinations by your veterinarian are essential to

Strong chewers like German Shepherds require strong chew devices. The Hercules™ by Nylabone® is a dental device which is made from very heavy polyurethane.

maintaining your dog's good health. If your veterinarian detects periodontal disease, he or she may recommend a prophylactic cleaning. To do a thorough cleaning, it will be necessary to put your dog under anesthesia. With modern gas anesthetics and monitoring equipment, the procedure is pretty safe. Your veterinarian will scale the teeth with an ultrasound scaler or hand instrument. This removes the calculus from the teeth. If there are calculus deposits below the gum line, the veterinarian will plane the roots to make them smooth. After all of the calculus has been removed, the teeth are polished with pumice in a polishing cup. If any medical or surgical treatment is needed, it is done at this time. The final step would be fluoride treatment and your follow-up treatment at home. If the

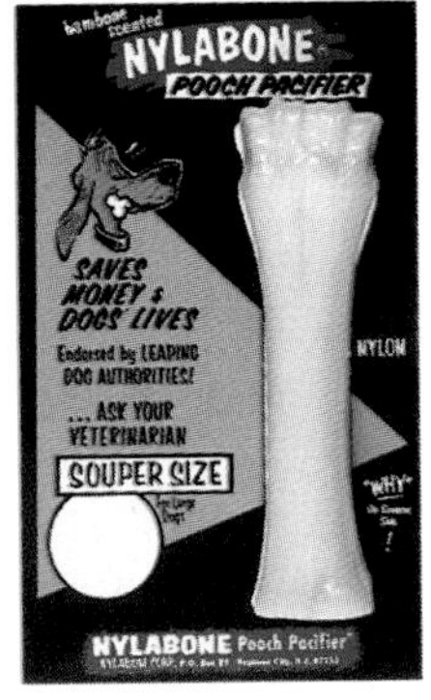

Nylabone® is highly recommended for German Shepherds by veterinarians as a safe, healthy nylon bone that can't splinter or chip. It is available at your local pet shop.

Made of durable and flexible polyurethane, the Gumabone® Frisbee® proves chew-worthy and good-smelling to dogs.*

**The trademark Frisbee is used under license from Mattel, Inc., California, USA.*

periodontal disease is advanced, the veterinarian may prescribe a medicated mouth rinse or antibiotics for use at home. Make sure your dog has safe, clean and attractive chew toys and treats. Chooz® treats are another way of using a consumable treat to help keep your dog's teeth clean.

Rawhide is the most popular of all materials for a dog to chew. This has never been good news to dog owners, because rawhide is inherently very dangerous for dogs. Thousands of dogs have died from rawhide, having swallowed the hide after it has become soft and mushy, only to cause stomach and intestinal blockage. A new rawhide product on the market has finally solved the problem of rawhide: molded Roar-Hide® from Nylabone. These are composed of processed, cut up, and melted American rawhide injected into your dog's favorite shape: a dog bone. These dog-safe devices smell and taste like rawhide but don't break up. The ridges on the bones help to fight tartar build-up on the teeth and they last ten times longer than the usual rawhide chews.

As your dog ages, professional examination and cleaning should become more frequent. The mouth should be inspected at least once a year. Your veterinarian may recommend visits every six months. In the geriatric patient, organs such as

Molded rawhide, called Roar-Hide™ by Nylabone® is very hard and safe for your dog. These devices smell and taste like rawhide but don't break up as quickly.

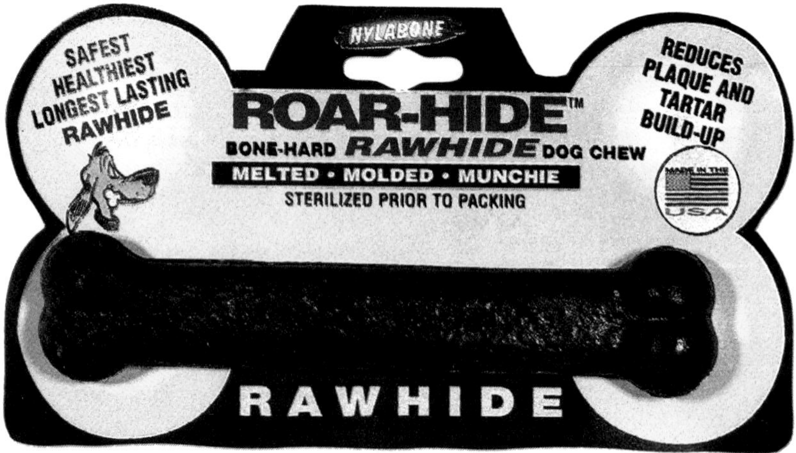

Chooz™ treats are another way of using a consumable treat to help keep your German Shepherd's teeth clean.

the heart, liver, and kidneys do not function as well as when they were young. Your veterinarian will probably want to test these organs' functions prior to using general anesthesia for dental cleaning. If your dog is a good chewer and you work closely with your veterinarian, your dog can keep all of its teeth all of its life. However, as your dog ages, his sense of smell, sight, and taste will diminish. He may not have the desire to chase, trap or chew his toys. He will also not have the energy to chew for long periods, as arthritis and periodontal disease make chewing painful. This will leave you with more responsibility for keeping his teeth clean and healthy. The dog that would not let you brush his teeth at one year of age, may let you brush his teeth now that he is ten years old.

If you train your dog with good chewing habits as a puppy, he will have healthier teeth throughout his life.

HEALTH CARE for Your Dog

Veterinary medicine has become far more sophisticated than what was available to our ancestors. This can be attributed to the increase in household pets and consequently the demand for better care for them. Also human medicine has become far more complex. Today diagnostic testing in veterinary medicine parallels human diagnostics. Because of better technology we can expect our pets to live healthier lives thereby increasing their life spans.

THE FIRST CHECK UP

You will want to take your new puppy/dog in for its first check up within 48 to 72 hours after acquiring it. Many breeders strongly recommend this check up and so do the humane shelters. A puppy/dog can appear healthy but it may have a serious problem that is not apparent to the layman. Most pets have some type of a minor

Until a puppy's immune system becomes functional, it receives all of the necessary antibodies via its mother's milk.

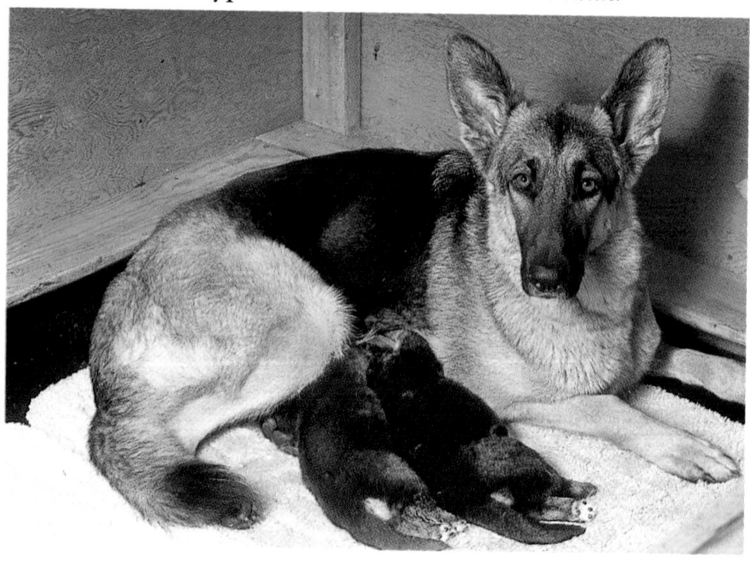

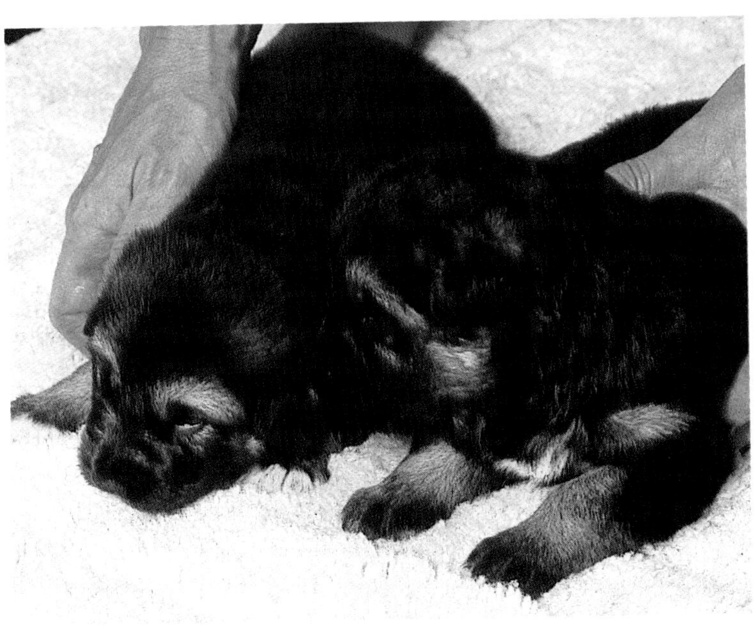

Until the puppies have received their first set of inoculations, only the breeder should be handling them.

flaw that may never cause a real problem.

Unfortunately if he/she should have a serious problem, you will want to consider the consequences of keeping the pet and the attachments that will be formed, which may be broken prematurely. Keep in mind there are many healthy dogs looking for good homes.

This first check up is a good time to establish yourself with the veterinarian and learn the office policy regarding their hours and how they handle emergencies. Usually the breeder or another conscientious pet owner is a good reference for locating a capable veterinarian. You should be aware that not all veterinarians give the same quality of service. Please do not make your selection on the least expensive clinic, as they may be short changing your pet. There is the possibility that eventually it will cost you more due to improper diagnosis, treatment, etc. If you are selecting a new veterinarian, feel free to ask for a tour of the clinic. You should inquire about making an

A young puppy's outdoor activity should be restricted to the yard until he is fully vaccinated.

appointment for a tour since all clinics are working clinics, and therefore may not be available all day for sightseers. You may worry less if you see where your pet will be spending the day if he ever needs to be hospitalized.

THE PHYSICAL EXAM

Your veterinarian will check your pet's overall condition, which includes listening to the heart; checking the respiration; feeling the abdomen, muscles and joints; checking the mouth, which includes the gum color and signs of gum disease along with plaque buildup; checking the ears for signs of an infection or ear mites; examining the eyes; and, last but not least, checking the condition of the skin and coat.

He should ask you questions regarding your pet's eating and elimination habits and invite you to relay your questions. It is a good idea to prepare a list so as not to forget anything. He should discuss the proper diet and the quantity to be fed. If this should differ from your breeder's recommendation, then you should convey to him the breeder's choice and see if he approves. If he recommends changing the diet, then this should be done over a few days so as not to cause a gastrointestinal upset. It is customary to take in a fresh stool sample (just a small amount) for a test for intestinal parasites. It must be fresh, preferably within 12 hours, since the eggs hatch quickly and after hatching will not be observed under the microscope. If your pet isn't obliging then, usually the technician can take one in the clinic.

Daily exercise is as much a part of your German Shepherd's good health as are trips to the veterinarian.

Immunizations

It is important that you take your puppy/ dog's vaccination record with you on your first visit. In case of a puppy, presumably the breeder has seen to the vaccinations up to the time you acquired custody. Veterinarians differ in their vaccination protocol. It is not unusual for your puppy to have received vaccinations for distemper, hepatitis, leptospirosis, parvovirus and parainfluenza every two to three weeks from the age of five or six weeks. Usually this is a combined injection and is typically called the DHLPP. The DHLPP is given through at least 12 to 14 weeks of age, and it is customary to continue with another parvovirus vaccine at 16 to 18 weeks. You may wonder why so many immunizations are necessary. No one knows for sure when the puppy's maternal antibodies are gone, although it is customarily accepted that distemper antibodies are gone by 12 weeks. Usually parvovirus antibodies are gone by 16 to 18 weeks of age.

However, it is possible for the maternal antibodies to be gone at a much earlier age or even a later age. Therefore immunizations are started at an early age. The vaccine will not give immunity as long as there are maternal antibodies.

The rabies vaccination is given at three or six months of age depending on your local laws. A vaccine for bordetella (kennel cough) is advisable and can be given anytime from the age of five weeks. The coronavirus is not commonly given unless there is a problem locally. The Lyme vaccine is necessary in endemic areas. Lyme disease has been reported in 47 states.

Your puppy's vaccination schedule should begin at six to eight weeks of age and continue until 14 to16 weeks of age; then he will be ready to face the world!

Distemper

This is virtually an incurable disease. If the dog recovers, he is subject to severe nervous disorders. The virus attacks every tissue in the body and resembles a bad cold with a fever. It can cause a runny nose and eyes and cause gastrointestinal disorders, including a poor appetite, vomiting and diarrhea. The virus is carried by raccoons, foxes, wolves, mink and other dogs. Unvaccinated youngsters and senior citizens are very susceptible. This is still a common disease.

Hepatitis

This is a virus that is most serious in very young dogs. It is spread by contact with an infected animal or its stool or urine. The virus affects the liver and kidneys and is characterized by high fever, depression and lack of appetite. Recovered animals may be afflicted with chronic illnesses.

Leptospirosis

This is a bacterial disease transmitted by contact with the urine of an infected dog, rat or other wildlife. It produces severe symptoms of fever, depression, jaundice and internal bleeding and was fatal before the vaccine was developed. Recovered dogs can be carriers, and the disease can be transmitted from dogs to humans.

Parvovirus

This was first noted in the late 1970s and is still a fatal disease. However, with proper vaccinations, early diagnosis and prompt treatment, it is a manageable disease. It attacks the bone marrow and intestinal tract. The symptoms include depression, loss of appetite, vomiting, diarrhea and collapse. Immediate medical attention is of the essence.

Rabies

This is shed in the saliva and is carried by raccoons, skunks, foxes, other dogs and cats. It attacks nerve tissue, resulting in paralysis and death. Rabies can be transmitted to people and is virtually always fatal. This disease is reappearing in the suburbs.

Bordetella (Kennel Cough)

The symptoms are coughing, sneezing, hacking and retching accompanied by nasal discharge usually lasting from a few days to several weeks. There are several disease-producing organisms responsible for this disease. The present vaccines are helpful but do not protect for all the strains. It usually is not life threatening but in some instances it can progress to a serious bronchopneumonia. The disease is highly contagious. The vaccination should be given routinely for dogs that come in contact with other dogs, such as through boarding, training class or visits to the groomer.

A reputable boarding kennel will require that dogs have received the vaccination for kennel cough within six months of their scheduled stay.

Coronavirus

This is usually self limiting and not life threatening. It was first noted in the late '70s about a year before parvovirus. The virus produces a yellow/brown stool and there may be depression, vomiting and diarrhea.

Lyme Disease

This was first diagnosed in the United States in 1976 in Lyme, CT in people who lived in close proximity to the deer tick. Symptoms may include acute lameness, fever, swelling of joints and loss of appetite. Your veterinarian can advise you if you live in an endemic area.

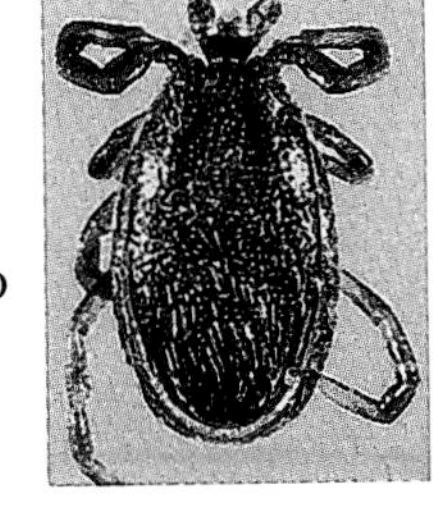

The deer tick is the most common carrier of Lyme disease. Your veterinarian can advise you if you live in an endemic area.

After your puppy has completed his puppy vaccinations, you will continue to booster the DHLPP once a year. It is customary to booster the rabies one year after the first vaccine and then, depending on where you live, it should be boostered every year or every three years. This depends on your local laws. The Lyme and corona vaccines are boostered annually and it is recommended that the bordetella be boostered every six to eight months.

Annual Visit

I would like to impress the importance of the annual check up, which would include the booster vaccinations, check for intestinal parasites and test for heartworm. Today in our very busy world it is rush, rush and see "how much you can get for how little." Unbelievably, some non-veterinary businesses have entered into the vaccination business. More harm than good can come to your dog through improper vaccinations, possibly from inferior vaccines and/or the wrong schedule. More than likely you truly care about your companion dog and over the years you have devoted much time and expense to his well being. Perhaps you are unaware that a vaccination is not just a vaccination. There is more involved. Please, please follow through with regular physical examinations. It is so important for your veterinarian to know your dog and this is especially true during middle age through the geriatric years. More than likely your older dog will require more than one physical a year. The annual physical is good preventive medicine. Through early diagnosis and subsequent treatment your dog can maintain a longer and better quality of life.

INTESTINAL PARASITES

Hookworms

These are an almost microscopic intestinal worms that can cause anemia and therefore serious problems, including death, in young puppies. Hookworms can be transmitted to humans through penetration of the skin. Puppies may be born with them.

Roundworms

These are spaghetti-like worms that can cause a potbellied appearance and dull coat along with more severe symptoms, such as vomiting, diarrhea and coughing. Puppies acquire these while in the mother's uterus and through lactation. Both hookworms and roundworms may be acquired through ingestion.

Whipworms

These have a three-month life cycle and are not acquired through the dam. They cause intermittent diarrhea usually with mucus. Whipworms are possibly the most difficult worm to eradicate. Their eggs are very resistant to most

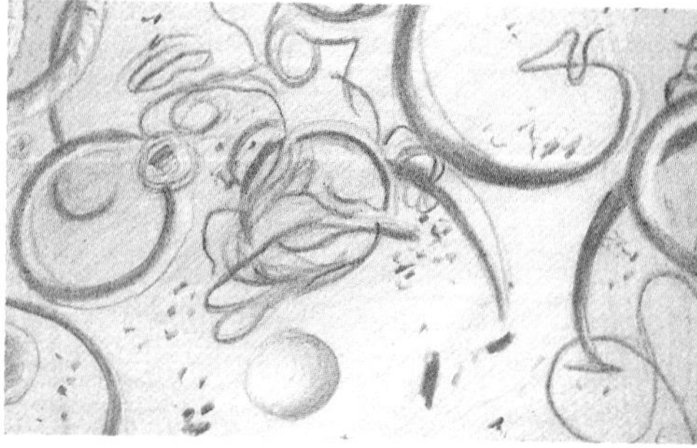

Adult whipworms. These are possibly the most difficult worm to eradicate.

environmental factors and can last for years until the proper conditions enable them to mature. Whipworms are seldom seen in the stool.

Roundworm eggs, as seen on a fecal evaluation. The eggs must develop for at least 12 days before they are infective.

Intestinal parasites are more prevalent in some areas than others. Climate, soil and contamination are big factors contributing to the incidence of intestinal parasites. Eggs are passed in the stool, lay on the ground and then become infective in a certain number of days. Each of the above worms has a different life cycle. Your best chance of becoming and remaining worm-free is to always pooper-scoop your yard. A fenced-in yard keeps stray dogs out, which is certainly helpful.

I would recommend having a fecal examination on your dog twice a year or more often if there is a problem. If your dog has a positive fecal sample, then he will be given the appropriate medication and you will be asked to bring back another stool sample in a certain period of time (depending on the type of worm) and then rewormed if necessary. This process goes on until he has at least two negative samples. The different types of worms require different medications. You will be wasting your money and doing your dog an injustice by buying over-the-counter medication without first consulting your veterinarian.

Other Internal Parasites

Coccidiosis and Giardiasis

These protozoal infections usually affect puppies, especially in places where large numbers of puppies are brought together. Older dogs may harbor these infections but do not show signs unless they are stressed. Symptoms include diarrhea, weight loss and lack of appetite. These infections are not always apparent in the fecal examination.

The cat flea is the most common flea of dogs. It starts feeding soon after it makes contact with the dog. Courtesy of Fleabusters, Rx for Fleas, Inc.

Tapeworms

Seldom apparent on fecal floatation, they are diagnosed frequently as rice-like segments around the dog's anus and the base of the tail. Tapeworms are long, flat and ribbon like, sometimes several feet in length, and made up of many segments about five-eighths of an inch long. The two most common types of tapeworms found in the dog are:

(1) First the larval form of the flea tapeworm parasite must mature in an intermediate host, the flea, before it can become infective. Your dog acquires this by ingesting the flea through licking and chewing.

(2) Rabbits, rodents and certain large game animals serve as intermediate hosts for other species of tapeworms. If your dog should eat one of these infected hosts, then he can acquire tapeworms.

HEARTWORM DISEASE

This is a worm that resides in the heart and adjacent blood vessels of the lung that produces microfilaria, which circulate in the bloodstream. It is possible for a dog to be infected with any number of worms from one to a hundred that can be 6 to 14 inches long. It is a life-threatening disease, expensive to treat and easily prevented. Depending on where you live, your veterinarian may recommend a preventive year-round and either an annual or semiannual blood test. The most common preventive is given once a month.

External Parasites

Fleas

These pests are not only the dog's worst enemy but also enemy to the owner's pocketbook. Preventing is less expensive than treating, but regardless I think we'd prefer to spend our money elsewhere. I would guess that the majority of our dogs are allergic to the bite of a flea, and in many cases it only takes one flea bite. The protein in the flea's saliva is the culprit. Allergic dogs have a reaction, which usually results in a "hot spot." More than likely such a reaction will involve a trip to the veterinarian for treatment. Yes, prevention is less expensive. Fortunately today there are several good products available.

If there is a flea infestation, no one product is going to correct the problem. Not only will the dog require treatment so will the

The best approach to prevent and eliminate flea infestation in the house is to use a safe insecticide. Courtesy of Fleabusters, Rx for Fleas, Inc.

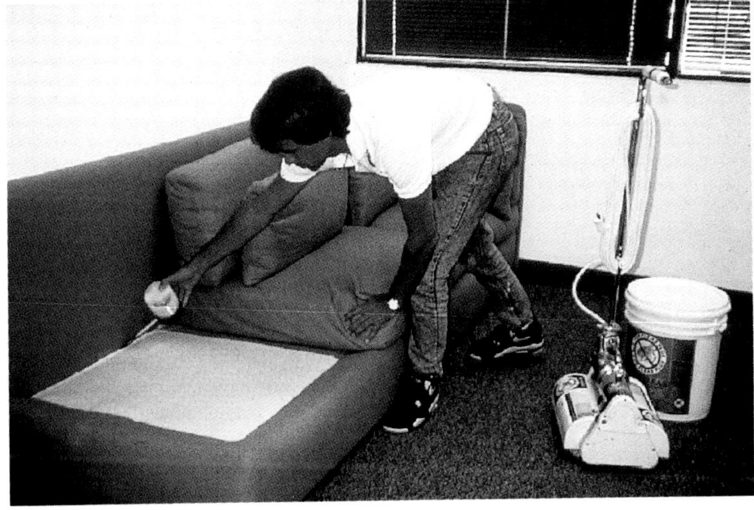

environment. In general flea collars are not very effective although there is now available an "egg" collar that will kill the eggs on the dog. Dips are the most economical but they are messy. There are some effective shampoos and treatments available through pet shops and veterinarians. An oral tablet arrived on the American market in 1995 and was popular in Europe the previous year. It sterilizes the female flea but will not kill adult fleas. Therefore the tablet, which is given monthly, will decrease the flea population but is not a "cure-all." Those dogs that suffer from flea-bite allergy will still be subjected to the bite of the flea. Another popular parasiticide is permethrin, which is applied to the back of the dog in one or two places depending on the dog's weight. This product works as a repellent causing the flea to get "hot feet" and jump off. Do not confuse this product with some of the organophosphates that are also applied to the dog's back.

Some products are not usable on young puppies. Treating fleas should be done under your veterinarian's guidance. Frequently it is necessary to combine products and the layman does not have the knowledge regarding possible toxicities. It is hard to believe but there are a few dogs that do have a natural resistance to fleas. Nevertheless it would be wise to treat all pets at the same time. Don't forget your cats. Cats just love to prowl the neighborhood and consequently return with unwanted guests.

Adult fleas live on the dog but their eggs drop off the dog into the environment. There they go through four larval stages before reaching adulthood, and thereby are able to jump back on the poor unsuspecting dog. The cycle resumes and takes between 21 to 28 days under ideal conditions. There are environmental products available

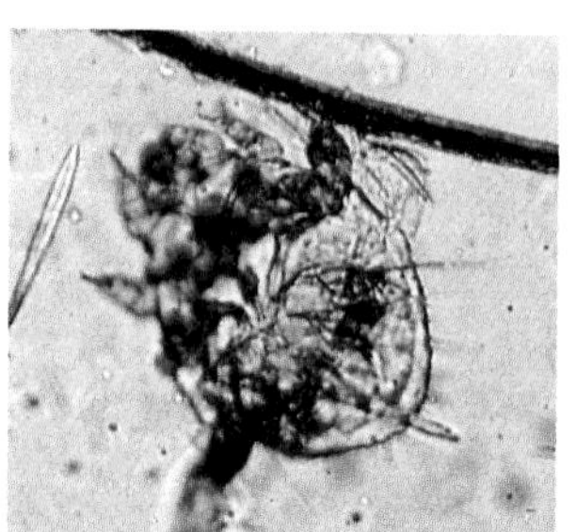

Sarcoptes are highly contagious to other dogs and to humans, although they do not live long on humans. They cause intense itching.

that will kill both the adult fleas and the larvae.

Ticks

Ticks carry Rocky Mountain Spotted Fever, Lyme disease and can cause tick paralysis. They should be removed with tweezers, trying to pull out the head. The jaws carry disease. There is a tick preventive collar that does an excellent job. The ticks automatically back out on those dogs wearing collars.

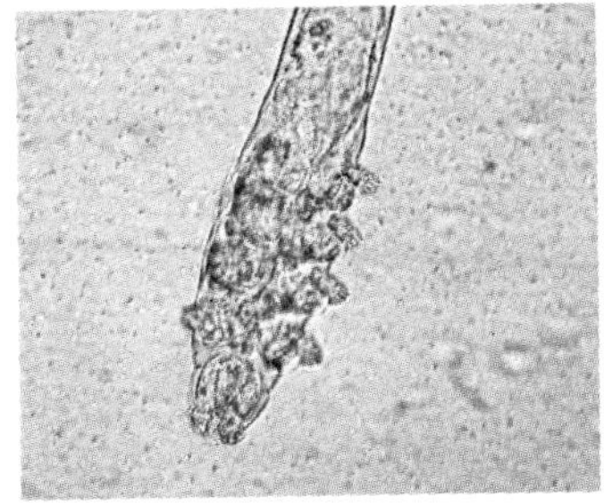

The demodex mite is passed from the dam to her puppies. It affects youngsters from the ages of three to ten months.

Sarcoptic Mange

This is a mite that is difficult to find on skin scrapings. The pinnal reflex is a good indicator of this disease. Rub the ends of the pinna (ear) together and the dog will start scratching with his foot. Sarcoptes are highly contagious to other dogs and to humans although they do not live long on humans. They cause intense itching.

Demodectic Mange

This is a mite that is passed from the dam to her puppies. It affects youngsters age three to ten months. Diagnosis is confirmed by skin scraping. Small areas of alopecia around the eyes, lips and/or forelegs become visible. There is little itching unless there is a secondary bacterial infection. Some breeds are afflicted more than others.

Cheyletiella

This causes intense itching and is diagnosed by skin scraping. It lives in the outer layers of the skin of dogs, cats, rabbits and humans. Yellow-gray scales may be found on the back and the rump, top of the head and the nose.

TO BREED OR NOT TO BREED

More than likely your breeder has requested that you have your puppy neutered or spayed. Your breeder's request is based on what is healthiest for your dog and what is most beneficial for your breed. Experienced and conscientious breeders devote many years into developing a bloodline. In order to do this, he makes every effort to plan each breeding in regard to conformation, temperament and health. This type of breeder does his best to perform the necessary testing (i.e., OFA, CERF, testing for inherited blood disorders, thyroid, etc.). Testing is expensive and sometimes very disheartening when a favorite dog doesn't pass his health tests. The health history pertains not only to the breeding stock but to the immediate ancestors. Reputable breeders do not want their offspring to be bred indiscriminately. Therefore you may be asked to neuter or spay your puppy. Of course there is always the exception, and your breeder may agree to let you breed your dog under his direct supervision. This is an important concept. More and more effort is being made to breed healthier dogs.

Spay/Neuter

There are numerous benefits of performing this surgery at six months of age. Unspayed females are subject to mammary and ovarian cancer. In order to prevent mammary cancer she must be spayed prior to

There are many unexpected problems when breeding dogs. These English Setter puppies were rejected by their dam and are being fostered by this male Shepherd.

her first heat cycle. Later in life, an unspayed female may develop a pyometra (an infected uterus), which is definitely life threatening.

Spaying is performed under a general anesthetic and is easy on the young dog. As you might expect it is a little harder on the older dog, but that is no reason to deny her the surgery. The surgery removes the ovaries and uterus. It is important to remove all the ovarian tissue. If some is left behind, she could remain attractive to males. In order to view the ovaries, a reasonably long incision is necessary. An ovariohysterectomy is considered major surgery.

Neutering the male at a young

Dogs that are neutered usually live longer, healthier lives because the risk of cancer of the reproductive organs is eliminated.

As pregnancy progresses, the bitch's abdomen will swell with the expanding uterus and her mammary glands will fill with milk. Regular inspections by the veterinarian should be scheduled, especially if she is a first-time mother.

age will inhibit some characteristic male behavior that owners frown upon. I have found my boys will not hike their legs and mark territory if they are neutered at six months of age. Also neutering at a young age has hormonal benefits, lessening the chance of hormonal aggressiveness.

Surgery involves removing the testicles but leaving the scrotum. If there should be a retained testicle, then he definitely needs to be neutered before the age of two or three years. Retained testicles can develop into cancer. Unneutered males are at risk for testicular cancer, perineal fistulas, perianal tumors and fistulas and prostatic disease.

Intact males and females are prone to housebreaking accidents. Females urinate frequently before, during and after heat cycles, and males tend to mark territory if there is a female in heat. Males may show the same behavior if there is a visiting dog or guests.

Surgery involves a sterile operating procedure equivalent to human surgery. The incision site is shaved, surgically scrubbed and draped. The veterinarian wears a sterile surgical gown, cap, mask and gloves. Anesthesia should be monitored by a registered technician. It is customary for the veterinarian to recommend a pre-anesthetic blood screening, looking for metabolic problems and a ECG rhythm strip to check for normal heart function. Today anesthetics are equal to human anesthetics, which enables your dog to walk out of the clinic the same day as surgery.

Some folks worry about their dog's gaining weight after being neutered or spayed. This is usually not the case. It is true that some dogs may be less active so they could develop a problem, but my own dogs are just as active as they were before surgery. I have a hard time keeping weight on them. However, if your dog should begin to gain, then you need to decrease his food and see to it that he gets a little more exercise.

SUGGESTED READING

TS-252
Dog Behavior and Training

TS-249
Skin & Coat Care for Your Dog

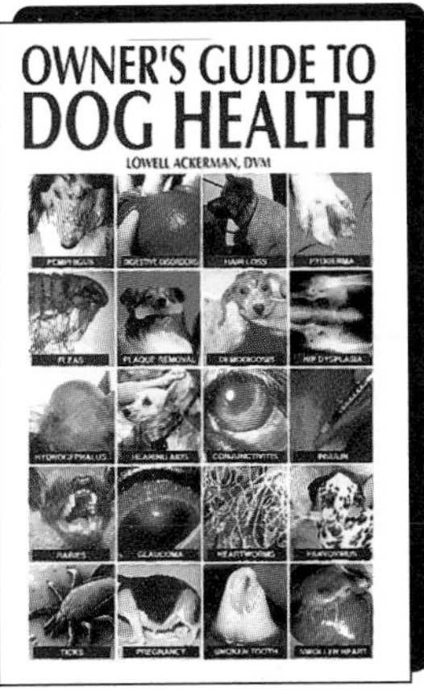

TS-214
Owner's Guide to Dog Health

TS-205
Successful Dog Training

TS-258
Training Your Dog For Sports and Other Activities

H-1062
Book of the German Shepherd Dog

PS-810
The German Shepherd Dog

INDEX

Agility, 126
Air travel, 132
Alsatian League and Club of Great Britain, 15
Alsatian Wolf Dog, 12, 14
American Kennel Club, 120
American Rescue Dog Association, 62
ASPCA, 135
Bathing, 102
Bed, 110
Bite, 30
Boarding kennels, 134
Body, 32
Bordetella, 148
Brayton, Nancy, 52
Breeders, 69
Breeding, 15, 156
Brushing, 101
Canadian Kennel Club, 120
Canine Good Citizen, 124
Car travel, 130
Chewing, 111
Cheyletiella, 155
Children, 98
Chooz, 140
Coat, 29
Coccidiosis, 151
Color, 27
Conformation showing, 122
Coronavirus, 149
Crate, 108, 130
Demodectic mange, 155
Description, 20
Development of puppies, 116
Distemper, 146
Ears, 30
Elimination, 96
English, Margaret, 54
Environment, 22
Exercise, 23, 96
Eyes, 30
Feeding, 92
Fleas, 153
Floating jaw, 32
Gait, 33
Galileo Bone, 137
German Shepherd Dog Club of America, 12, 16
German Shepherd Dog, its History, Development and Genetics, 10
German Shepherd Dog, The, 19
Giardiasis, 151
Goldbecker, William, 19
Grooming, 101
Guide dogs, 46
Gumabone®, 76, 138
Hart, Ernest H., 19
Head, 30
Heartworm, 152
Heaven, Stephen, 48
Hektor Linksrhein, 9
Hektor v. Schwaben, 10, 12
Hepatitis, 146
Hercules Bone, 138
Hip dysplasia, 16
Hookworms, 150
Horand v. Grafrath, 10
Housing, 107
Humane Society of the United States, 133
Immunizations, 145
Intermountain Search and Rescue Dog Association, 59
Junior Showmanship, 124
Kennel Club, The, 120
Kennel cough, 148
Kindergarten classes, 118
Langendoen, Bob, 59
Lavoie, Sue, 59
Leptospirosis, 146
Lyme disease, 149
Microchipping, 128
Mira v. Offingen, 12
Monorchidism, 6
Mores Plieningen, 10
Nails, 103
Name, 12
National Association of Professional Pet Sitters, 135
Neutering, 73, 156
Nicholas, Anna Katherine, 19
Nylabone®, 76, 103, 138
Nylafoss®, 137
Obedience, 125
–training, 118
Orthopedic Foundation for Animals, 16
Parasites, 150
Parker, Melissa, 64
Parvovirus, 148
Pedigrees, 70, 89
Periodontal disease, 138
Phylax Society, 9
Physical appearance, 27
Physical exam, 144
Plaque Attackers, 137
Protectiveness, 22
Purchasing, 66, 71, 88
–age, 74
–sex, 72
–sources, 71
Rabies, 148
Rawhide, 140
Register of Merit, 16
Registration, 82
Riser, Wayne, 16
Roar-Hide, 140
Roundworms, 150
Sarcoptic mange, 155
Schedule, 112
Schutzhund, 127
Search and Rescue dogs, 47
Seeing Eye dogs, 15
Selection, 66, 84
Shedding, 101
Socialization, 78
Spaying, 73, 156
Tapeworms, 152
Tattooing, 128
Teeth, 30, 103
–brushing, '37
–cleaning, 139, 140
–professional examination, 140
This is the German Shepherd, 19
Ticks, 155
Tipton, Keith, 50
Touring with Touser, 132
Tracking, 126
Training, 104, 118
Traveling with Your Pet, 135
Verein fur Deutsche Schaferhunde, 10
Veterinarian, 142
–annual visit, 149
–first visit, 142
von Stephanitz, Max, 9
War messengers, 15, 46
Water, 93
Weight, 32
Whipworms, 150
Willis, Malcom, 11
World of the German Shepherd Dog, The, 19
World War I, 11, 12